Mental Health Tips

Because Mental Health Matters

Kelly J Bawden, MS, LMFT

BALBOA.
PRESS

A DIVISION OF HAY HOUSE

This is a book of mental health tips to help you improve and repair your life. Life is hard, and many times our emotions and negative thinking patterns get in the way of effectively handling problems. This book offers tips to improve negative thinking patterns, decrease emotional stress, improve communication to others, improve relationships not only with others but with yourself as well, and to stop self-destructive behaviors so you can improve your overall life. The tools within this book are designed to help you get in charge of your life.

Balboa Press books may be ordered through booksellers or by contacting:

Balboa Press
A Division of Hay House
1663 Liberty Drive
Bloomington, IN 47403
www.balboapress.com
1 (877) 407-4847

Print information available on the last page.

ISBN: 978-1-5043-4476-0 (sc)
ISBN: 978-1-5043-4478-4 (hc)
ISBN: 978-1-5043-4477-7 (e)

Library of Congress Control Number: 2015918581

Balboa Press rev. date: 1/25/2016

Contents

Acknowledgments

Talking about mental health is still taboo; however, if we do not take care of our mental health, it can affect our life without our even knowing it. I did not realize how much not dealing with the grief from losing my son was affecting how I was living my life. Because of my daughter and grandchildren, I was motivated to do something about it. I am grateful for family, friends, counselors, and mentors who helped me. I am grateful to be able to write about mental health and pass on what I have learned through my own journey and the journey of those I have been privileged to work with. I am humbled by what so many have endured in their lives. It is important for all of us to remember that mental health matters.

Chapter 1

Mental Health Tip #1: Whether you believe
you can or can't, you are right ... so in
this moment, believe in yourself.

My first mental health tip is about learning to have a relationship with yourself. Most people are pretty hard on themselves. Negative self-talk will tear down your confidence and ability to take risks and achieve your goals. Many times we use distractions to feel better. These distractions are usually self-destructive and allow us to hide how we are truly feeling. This keeps us from taking risks in life. It is often easier to tell ourselves why we cannot do something than it is to risk and challenge ourselves.

When we first imagine a goal or dream, there are no judgments or conflicts in our imagination. There is only the vision of what achieving that goal or dream will look like. But once it has been imagined, doubts start entering our minds. These thoughts may sound like this: "I do not have the money to do this," "I don't have the education or ability to pull this off," "I am not good enough," "I am not worth it," or "This is a stupid dream. Why would I ever pursue it?" The list goes on and on. Our past and what we think about ourselves determine if we will begin taking steps toward our goal or stay stuck by believing those awful thoughts and maintaining the status quo.

It is very common for people to doubt their abilities, wish for a different life, and continue an unsatisfactory life. They complain of being bored and stressed-out most of the time and often turn to self-destructive behaviors to ease the pain, such as drinking alcohol daily, overusing prescription medications, gambling away their money, viewing pornography, spending money they do not have, or overeating or binge-eating to avoid feeling low. These behaviors become patterns that are very hard to change. Often these behaviors become addictions. Life then becomes a series of cycles and patterns that just do not feel good. This creates low moods, anxiety, depression, and feelings of overwhelm and frustration.

Listening to these negative thoughts and the reasons that something is impossible only increases self-doubt and negative thinking. Affirmations go both ways. If we listen to our negative self-talk, we affirm these negative thoughts. Henry Ford once said, "Whether you think you can or you can't, you are right." This is absolutely true. What we tell ourselves shapes our lives. If our thoughts are filled with self-doubt, our actions will continue to bring consequences that will affirm our self-doubt. It becomes a vicious cycle.

There are so many problems in life that it can feel overwhelming. People from all backgrounds have challenges in life. When drink, gambling, food, pills, or other addictions become the way to cope with stress, it actually increases the stress. People may feel relief in the moment, but it does not last long.

Mental health is not talked about very often. I would love to help change that, and this book is my way to help people know that mental health is a part of life and it's good to talk about it. It is actually *healing* to talk about it. I have a passion for mental health and have seen so many lives disrupted because of self-destructive behaviors. In my 20 years of counseling clients I have learned many tools that improve mental health. I have an extensive educational background in marriage and family therapy, mental health therapy, and psychology. I am currently working on a PhD in psychology. Most of the tools I teach come from not only my education, but also my life experiences.

I have seen many people who have gambled away their money or were financially successful but used methamphetamine, cocaine, or other illicit drugs to get through the day. I have counseled with people who drank themselves to the point of passing out every night and those who have abused prescription pills to the point that they were not the same person. I have worked with those who ate as a way to decrease stress but in the end felt sick because they had eaten so much. At the time, it feels like the food, alcohol, or drug is helping, but in the end, it is making things worse. We can't eat away our emotions, drink away our problems, or use pills as a coping mechanism.

Drugs and alcohol change people. I am not referring to social drinking or drinking to celebrate an event. I am talking about the drug and alcohol use that affects an individual's entire life. I have worked with many individuals whose lives have fallen apart because of drugs or alcohol. I have also worked with individuals who have continued to function and keep their jobs or their relationships intact. We each have a story that we live every day.

Patty was successful, but she had been drinking, gambling, and using cocaine and Adderall for about fifteen years. By the time she reached midlife, she really had nothing to show for it and a hard time remembering most of it. She had a grown child, but she didn't remember most of his life. When her son had a child of his own, this spurred her to think about life a little differently. She began

Kelly J Bawden, MS, LMFT

looking at her life and felt a lot of regret. She realized how lonely she was most of the time. She was successful in business, but it was not enough. She would get up and go to work, and after work, she would go drink and gamble. She used cocaine or Adderall to get through the day, and in the evening, she would drink until she passed out so she could sleep. However, she was passing out, not sleeping. In like manner, she was existing, not living.

When people exist instead of live, there is generally a great deal of self-destruction occurring. In the beginning, they may use drugs, alcohol, food, sex, or gambling as a way to deal with stress or to have some fun. But eventually, these patterns take over and become the coping skills they use to get through the day. These behaviors numb emotion and thus allow people to keep from feeling life. The behaviors also keep them from experiencing life, and when any emotion or discomfort occurs, the only way they know to deal with it is by drowning it in alcohol, prescription pills, sex, and so on. This can cause people to fear feeling the slightest emotion, and when they have not felt anything for a very long time, using drugs, alcohol, and food is a way to keep the emotion away. They fear the overwhelming hurt and pain; most of them never want to feel that way again. So drugs and alcohol cover up this emotion as well as other emotions. After feeling no emotions for so long, most people are not sure that they ever want to feel again.

The last time Patty felt anything was so painful that she vowed to never feel like that again. So drinking, using drugs, and gambling was her way to avoid it. The unbearable pain was the start of her destructive behaviors. The drinking helped her avoid feeling anything at night, using drugs helped her get through the stress of the day, and gambling was a way to escape the feeling of being alone. *How can I be alone if I am in a room full of people?* she thought. And it worked for years—until it didn't work anymore.

Once people get tired of being tied down to alcohol, drugs, or gambling, they begin to get tired of just existing and not feeling anything. Life then stops working, and the feeling of being alone starts creeping in. Sometimes people get tired of a life of self-destruction and not having anything pleasurable. There is no enjoyment in life, and this gets old. The only relationships they have are with alcohol and drugs. Then the realization that there is no one who really cares begins to creep in. The only people who seem to care are those who are providing the drugs.

If people are functioning in their jobs and are using, they probably isolate and are somewhat moody. Those who can keep a job do so because there is no need to have any closeness with people at work, as the job may not require extensive communication with others. Once this lifestyle takes over, it is very difficult to stop. Once the brain and the body have become addicted to the alcohol, drugs, gambling, or even food, the road to recovery is very difficult. Many people want to change their lives, but the first few years are so overwhelming that many go back to what made them feel better in the past, which was alcohol, drugs, food, or gambling.

When someone begins the process of recovery, it goes like this. Once alcohol and drugs are stopped, withdrawal begins, which can include nausea, headaches, achiness, muscle pain, and difficulty with sleeping, weight, and eating. Sugar then becomes the go-to. The body feels as though it were hit by a train.

Functioning for a long time while using alcohol and drugs can make it extremely difficult to learn to function without them. Patty was able to keep a good job even though she was drinking and using. In fact, drinking and drugs were what kept her functioning. Learning a new way to deal with life can take all the energy a person has to continue to function in the beginning stages of recovery or change.

For some people it can take over thirty-five days before they can sleep; it can take about ten days before the nausea and crawling skin stop. Being hit by a train may seem easier. Sometimes it can take about thirty days to feel anything, and then when it happens, the floodgates can open up and the crying begins, and then anger starts, and a person feels exhausted all the time. These new emotions that have been buried for so long are surfacing, and the feeling of living begins. The thoughts of wanting and deserving to have a good relationship also begin. Reconnection to family will be sought. Talking to other people will also begin, and learning once again how to connect to others and talk about life will be necessary. I have seen the genuineness in smiles when a life begins to change. The feelings of anger and depression are a challenge, but continuing to learn about life becomes important. At times everything can be okay, but the next moment the anger will come for no apparent reason. There will be times when anger will make a person do things like beat up his or her car or someone else's, throw books or TV remotes, or hit a wall. I once heard a story of someone who got so angry that while he was cooking dinner, the entrée became a punching bag, and after he cooked it he said it was the best dinner he had ever made. I love this story because it shows just how life is. Life is quite messy, and sometimes the enjoyment from life comes in the smallest of moments. The opportunity to listen to this story of struggle and triumph is the part of life that is genuine and real.

What does this have to do with believing in yourself? It has a lot to do with it. First, when someone is dealing with substance abuse or alcohol or food addictions, or in many cases all of these problems at once, the brain has been hijacked by sugar, drugs, and alcohol, and it is very difficult to recover from. The last thing someone can imagine is his or her brain not working properly, but the brain is in a sense broken. Since addiction is a disease of the brain, it is extremely difficult to not only understand but also to change the way the brain has been thinking. When the brain is diseased with an addiction, the part of the brain that is doing the thinking is the part that also deals with survival. This means that the part of the brain that makes all executive decisions is no longer making decisions because the survival part of the brain has taken over and is only thinking about the drug or alcohol or sugar it needs to survive. What this has to do with believing in oneself is that nobody could overcome addiction or recover from addiction if he or she did not believe he or she could.

Second, when you are using drugs, alcohol, sex, gambling, money, work, anger, or food to feel better, you are masking who you are. What you value about life is being overlooked. What you value within yourself is being masked and hidden by drugs, alcohol, and other self-destructive substances. All humans have these beliefs, and these beliefs are connected to what you value in life. These values are different for everyone and can come from our family, experiences, and our spiritual awareness. Some may value relationships, others may value family, and still others may value their creativity. When you go against your value system, you also need to cover up the hurt and pain, guilt and shame, and frustration that come from going against your values. You cover up these feelings by drinking, eating, spending money, sexual behaviors like viewing pornography, gambling, anger, and isolation. These are a few of the behaviors that become self-destructive and are used to feel numb; this allows us to keep focus on the outside (external pleasures) instead of the inside. This becomes a cycle, which then becomes a way of life.

The stories of people using drugs, alcohol, and other destructive substances are examples of keeping the focus off life. These behaviors are ways to avoid problems, hurt, guilt, and shame, and stay numb. Once someone begins to be aware of how numbing these behaviors are and how much avoidance hurts life, this can become the motivation and determination to change his or her life. Once someone begins to believe in oneself, life begins to change. The road is not an easy one, and since life is a journey, the only way to change the journey of your life is to believe you can. Take small steps toward the changes you want. Remember Henry Ford's words: "Whether you think you can or you can't, you are right."

Learn to believe in yourself by setting small goals and then taking the necessary steps to achieve them. Take a risk, and if you fall, get back up, brush yourself off, and do it all again. If you look back on your life and think about learning to ride a bike, catch a ball, swim, or write in cursive, it all took practice. The practice it took to be able to learn how to do these things is the same practice it will take to learn how to change your life. When we are children, it is easier to keep trying. Most kids are not second-guessing whether or not they can learn to write in cursive or learn to multiply; they just keep practicing until they can do it. The same concept applies to setting goals and living the life you want to live. When you get up in the morning, what is one thing you would like to accomplish? It may be something small like deep-clean the kitchen or something big like starting to write the novel you have always wanted to write. Whatever you want to accomplish that day, do it! Nothing gets accomplished unless there is action put toward the goal. Take the risk, and take the steps; it is worth it.

Belief in yourself comes from stopping self-destructive behavior, honoring your values and your life, and doing something every day to improve your life. If you value knowledge but you do not read or do anything to learn about things you love to learn about, you will probably find other ways to fill your time up. Most of the time this is where excessive sex, alcohol, gambling, drugs, food, or playing Xbox or online games comes in, and these behaviors can become excessive. If you have an excessive behavior you would like to get under control or you are amazed that the whole weekend went by and you didn't leave your home because you played online games, it may be time to reevaluate your life. Many people avoid life, become bored, and use gaming systems, social media, alcohol, or any other distraction to get rid of their boredom.

One way to decrease boredom is by doing something you are passionate about. Whether it is reading, music, art, or gardening you love, let yourself do these things. Set up a goal for something you enjoy doing and take steps toward the goal. If you feel like the weekend is the only time you have to do something like this, then plan time during your weekend to take a step on your goal. If you have thought about running a 5k, then start running for ten to twenty minutes on the weekend and work your way up to a few miles. You will be shocked at how your life will change just by changing one thing. If you would like your life to change, you have to change something. If you continue to live the same way doing the same thing day after day, your life will stay the same.

When you begin to take risks and do something every day that puts you one step closer to the goal, you begin to believe that you can do it. This belief begins to grow, and you start remembering who you are and what you value in life. Your life will start to change. You may actually wake up in the morning feeling a little excited about what the day will bring instead of waking up dreading the day ahead. When you begin to reach your goals, it helps you remember what you value about life. When you begin to live what you value, it becomes harder to go back to the old behaviors because these behaviors no longer satisfy or distract you. You will begin to feel better and plan life instead of just existing and following the same old road. Believe in yourself, and remember that you are worth it!

Chapter 2

Mental Health Tip #2: Getting to know and
like yourself can change your entire life.

What do you know about yourself? I am sure you know things like the foods you love or do not like, the activities you love to do, if you believe in a religion or higher power, or do not believe there is anything after this life. I am sure you know your favorite color, who your best friend is, and what your favorite pair of jeans is. These are all part of the external world in which we live. Knowing what your favorite things are or what you believe about the world around you comes from your experiences, the environment in which you live, and your social and familial circles.

We learn some of our beliefs from our family. When we are younger, we tend to believe the same things that our parents do. As we get older, our beliefs begin to change. They change because of our friends and because of what we learn in school; they change because of what we see in the media and the music we listen to. They change because of the events that happen in life or the peers that we hang out with. We may also change depending on our career path or whom we work for and work with. All of this change is happening because of the influences in our lives. Changes happen in life whether we want them to or not.

Charles R. Swindoll said, "We cannot change the past, we cannot change the way other people act, there is one thing that is inevitable and that is change." Change is going to happen whether we like it or not. Learning to ride the waves of change can make life a beautiful, twisted journey. To again quote Swindoll, "Our life is 10% what happens to us and 90% how we react to it." What have you done with the events in your life? Have you let these events change your outlook on life? Have these events created a negative attitude? Have these events inspired and motivated you? These are the decisions you get to make. You get to decide how the events in your life will influence you.

As all of the influences change the way we think and feel about life, we begin to get caught up in these things. We get caught up in what other people think, the clothing we wear, the type of car or truck we have, money—the lack of it or making more, finding the perfect man or woman, the way our body looks or the way we wish it looked, antiaging and making sure nobody can tell how old we are, the best electronics, homes, boats, motorcycles, vacations, and a million other things. If you do not have these things, then you spend time wishing you could have them and scheming to find a way to get them. Because of all these material influences, there is a tendency to lose the ability to know who you are and what you really value.

Values are the pieces of our self that help us decide to give to those who have less, help out friends when they are in need, help out Mom or Dad when they are sick, stay late at work to finish a project, help out someone on the side of the road with a flat tire, or apologize when we have lied to someone and don't feel good about it. Values are what keep us from doing things that would hurt others—or when we do hurt someone else, values help us make amends to that person. Values are that feeling that we did something good or we did something bad.

If you lied to someone to help your own career and it hurt another's career, you might walk away feeling bad about the lie. If you go back and tell the truth, you may feel better but lose the step up in your career. Whether you let the external, materialistic world be more important or your internal values be more important is how you will decide what to do. This is in part because your value system is telling you that stepping on someone's toes to get ahead does not feel right and the step up in the job is not worth what it would do to how you would feel about yourself.

Many individuals will ignore the internal self-talk and go with hurting someone else as well as themselves. The more that people hurt themselves and others to get what they want or get ahead, the more their relationship to themselves becomes damaged. Once the relationship to self is damaged, a person will look for other ways to feel better—for example, alcohol, drugs, sex, shopping, money, food, or gambling. The problem is that these things only provide short-term relief, and once the effect wears off, those who have used these external habits as coping mechanisms are still stuck with the way they feel about themselves. Instant gratification is used to feel better and to avoid thinking about the mistakes that have been made or the people who have been hurt.

When the outside world has become the focus in your life, there is a tendency to lose what you value, and so you do things that you would not normally do. You have lost a piece of who you are, and knowing who you are becomes clouded under all of the outside influences such as clothing, cell phones, cars, electronics, boats, ATVs, and other outside influences. These things are what our world and society tell us are important, and these worldly things become the most important part of your life, which makes it easier to go against your own values. The relationship you have with yourself is ignored or avoided; it is essentially put on a shelf and ignored.

For some reason the focus of life has become all about the external world and the things we have, the way we look, and how we look to other people. In the end, none of these things will really matter. What does matter is the relationship you have with yourself—how you view yourself and whether you are living in alignment with your values. These values are part of who you are. Are you letting go of what you believe and value to have something that gives you status with your friends? This does not mean you should never have something that you want; it means that if you are forgoing your own values to have something that will give you satisfaction in the moment, then instant gratification is determining the way you live. As in the previous chapter, when we forgo our own values, we tend to find an unhealthy behavior to help us become numb so we don't have to think about it or deal with it. This is how we avoid and say to ourselves that it does not matter. Only it does matter.

Getting to know and like yourself is not an easy task. First, you may have to spend time alone without any distractions to get a glimpse of who you are; and second, you may have to deal with many issues you have buried. One question to ask yourself is this: If you took away all of your belongings and you were by yourself without music or any other distractions, what would be left? Would you like spending time with you? Would you like the person you are? Would you have regrets or resentments? Would you want a distraction to stop the guilt or aggravation for something you did to get something you wanted? Would you begin to feel bad about something you did to someone else? What would be left is you with your thoughts, and these thoughts may be thoughts that you have tried to avoid for a long time. Taking some time to spend alone with you and your thoughts is a good way to check on how you are living.

Once you begin to take time to be with yourself, you then have to deal with these thoughts, memories, and emotions. This can become extremely challenging. The last thing most of us want to do is think about mistakes, big or small. Here is the reality: we all make mistakes and we all try to hide them; most of the time we hide these mistakes out of embarrassment or shame. Both of these emotions are difficult to deal with, so these emotions get covered up with distractions from the outside world instead of being dealt with. The only problem with this is that guilt and shame grow, and the more you try to cover up these feelings, the more these feelings come back with a vengeance later. You can't escape your mistakes, and you can't drown them in alcohol or food; sometimes you have to face the mistakes and start fixing things that you have done. It is scary to talk to someone that you hurt or apologize for something you did, but most of the time, most people are forgiving and appreciate the acknowledgment of your mistake.

Someone once told me that if I could not be alone with my thoughts, I needed to work on my relationship with myself. Now this was something I had never thought of. I had relationships with other people, my children, my friends, my coworkers, and my neighbors. I never thought about having a relationship with myself. I began thinking about this statement and started asking some difficult questions. I started thinking about the way I treated myself too. I found out I was very hard on myself. I needed to be a certain weight, and if I was not this weight, I would go on a cleanse that only allowed me to drink a certain juice for three to five days. Once when I really wanted to lose weight, I did this cleanse for ten days. I told people I was doing it to clean out my body and better my health, but the underlying reason was to lose weight. I did this to continue to look a certain way and keep up appearances, what I thought was expected of me. I wanted and needed to look perfect. Which also meant that I could not let anyone know I struggled with weight and binge eating, I would binge-eat when I was stressed or mad about something. I would binge-eat when nobody was home, which allowed me to keep it secret, and then use juice cleanses as a way to lose the weight. I kept this a secret for a very long time, and this secret kept me sick. I kept other secrets too. I did things financially to get what I thought was important, again to keep up appearances. I would justify it and make excuses, but I was never accountable for my actions I just kept spending money. I was working, raising children, and living in an unhealthy relationship.

I was selling real estate while my children were young, which allowed me to schedule my day around their activities. While I was selling real estate, I also worked at a health club because I had to keep up appearances even if it meant working a lot and running up credit cards to do it. I would tell myself that the next house sale would pay it off, and this became a financial cycle. I knew I was digging a hole, but I could not stop. I used spending and binge eating as a way to deal with my life, but neither of these coping methods would ever help me deal with the stressors of life or the way I felt about myself.

As I began examining my life, I could not help but wonder what I was doing. I put a lot of pressure on myself and my kids. I wanted them to excel in sports and dance, and I wanted them to get good grades. I always thought I was being supportive, but as I looked at what I was doing, the pressure I put on them was just an outlet of how I really felt about myself. What it did for them was create a reason for them to make up stories or act out in some way. I taught my kids how to blame others for why their grades were suffering or why they were acting out. I had lost what was really important in life; instead, I made how other people saw me and my kids important, only they really didn't know the real me. Other people only knew the image I presented to them. This image I tried to present was of someone who had it all together, who did not need help, and who knew it all. I laugh now even as I write this because I had things so backward.

When I began to realize what I was doing, I knew it was time to make a change. I had to let go of having to look perfect. I had to let go of having material things that didn't mean anything and didn't bring happiness into my life. I remember getting a new car and thinking that now I could enjoy life and be happy, but after a week of owning the car, I found myself having those same old feelings—a longing for something else. I would think about the next big purchase or something I really wanted, which would only frustrate me and so I would eat to make it all go away. By the time I was done eating, I felt worse than before, so the next day I would go out and buy everything to do a juice cleanse. What a crazy cycle, huh? I decided that it was time to learn to be honest with myself and learn who I was and what I stood for.

I remember the day I realized I was in a financial crisis, everything fell apart; I cried uncontrollably for what seemed like hours. I realized I needed to be accountable for my actions, for the debt I had gotten into. I needed to learn to be more open and ask for help. I needed to quit making excuses and blaming others for the reason we were in this kind of debt. I needed to be honest about why I cleansed and why I needed my kids to get good grades, excel in sports, and be popular in school. All of these things were because of what I lacked in my life. I always wanted to be the popular one, be good at sports, and be outgoing. What I really was, was shy, introverted, stubborn, and someone who cared deeply for my family and close friends. I just wanted to be different. I guess I wanted my kids to be everything I was not, so I pushed them to excel, especially when it came to sports and school activities.

It was time to stop. Over the next several months, I sold my truck and bought a car that would allow me to own it free and clear and pay off a credit card. Now this car was not what I was used to driving, and my kids called it the cream puff since it was the color of a cream puff. I quit using credit cards to buy things; if I didn't have the cash, I didn't buy it. I started asking my kids what they wanted to do instead of telling them what they should want. I started being accountable for my actions and quit blaming others for my actions. I became responsible for my life and my actions, and it felt good.

One of the hardest things to do is learn to be accountable for yourself. Accountability is facing all of your actions knowing that you made all of the choices. All of your actions are yours, and nobody made you do them. I used to blame police if I got a ticket. I would blame a teacher if my child was getting in trouble. I would blame the store when something broke and I still had to pay for it. I would buy what I wanted even if I didn't have money, and then I would get upset when the bill came in and I had to figure out how to pay it. Most of the time, I didn't have money for what I bought, but I would figure it out and our friends never knew that I was not as wealthy as they may have thought. The only thing I thought others knew was that I had the appearance of money. The fact was, I was mostly broke, lived check to check, and spent money I didn't have.

I spent money because I was avoiding the way I felt about myself. I wanted to be something different than I really was, and I wanted to be seen as equal to the friends we hung out with. I didn't want to be accountable; I wanted my problems to be somebody else's fault. Spending all this money would allow me to look like I had it all together. My problems were my problems only; nobody made me make these choices. I continued to make the same wrong choices. The result of this was financial problems, stress about the monthly bills, and always wanting something more than I had.

When I think back on the stress of my life and how much pressure I always felt, I am not sure how I got through it. I remember trying to sleep at night, and all I could think of was how was I going to pay for the cruise or how was I going to pay all the bills this month. I would try to figure out how to rotate money by getting another credit card. Eventually the pressure became too much, and I would eat to get relief.

Being accountable for my actions takes constant awareness. In the morning it is essential to do a self-check, asking myself some hard questions about my recent actions. Am I proud of what I did the day before? Did I avoid using food or spending money? Did I hurt anyone intentionally or unintentionally? Did I lie or blame someone else for what is happening in my life? What am I grateful for? Have I given back in some way to others? These questions will help you connect to you. Learning to self-reflect and evaluate your life is a good practice to have. Asking yourself the hard questions and being honest about your actions will improve your overall life.

These questions are just a few of the questions that can help you learn about who you are and what is important to you. Growth is a difficult process, and in that moment when you're growing, it may not feel all that great. I think this is where the old saying "What doesn't kill you will make you stronger" came from. To grow and expand is painful and uncomfortable; it can hurt, but it is simply uncomfortable and hurts in a good way. It may feel like your heart is going to explode or that your emotions are out of control. Remember that all of the pain that you go through to grow is part of this process. Learning about who you are and then being okay with that person is a journey. Gaining a relationship with yourself is the most important relationship. This relationship determines how all of your other relationships are. If you can't respect yourself, then how will you ever be able to respect someone else or get someone to respect you? The way you treat other people is a direct reflection of how you feel about yourself. If you don't like being in a room without any distractions, just you and your thoughts, you may have work to do. This journey is tough, but so very worth it.

Chapter 3

Mental Health Tip #3: Teach others how you would like to be treated. To do this, start by treating yourself like you would your best friend.

The way others treat you is directly related to the way you feel about and treat yourself. Now this is not always the case, especially in situations of abuse. In an abusive relationship, the power and control cycle that is happening feels like you can't do anything right even though you are trying. You may be feeling as though you are always walking on eggshells. If you have or are experiencing some type of abuse, seek out help from someone you can trust. Remember that you do not deserve the abuse, and more than likely, even though the abuser keeps telling you he or she will change, the probability of that happening is very low. Please seek help if you are experiencing abuse.

For most relationships, we teach others how to treat us. This may sound like a weird concept, but as you read this chapter, you may want to reflect on how you treat yourself and compare it to how others treat you; you may see some similarities. Looking at life as though each person in your life is somehow a reflection of a part of you will help you see into your own relationship with yourself. Understanding this can help you gain empathy and compassion for yourself and others. As you read through this chapter, reflect on those you are close to, those whom you get easily frustrated with, and those whom you tend to push away. This is all information for your own life, how you interact with others, and how you teach people to treat you.

Here is the reason that the way others treat you is a reflection of how you treat yourself. Suppose that you feel pretty good about who you are and you just met a man or woman who you think could be someone you could see yourself with. In the beginning it feels new and exciting, and the little quirks each of you have go unnoticed. You agree with this person on things you would not normally agree on, but this ensures that you won't lose him or her. This person begins to tell you he or she will call at a certain time, but then doesn't call. He or she takes you to places that are uncomfortable for you, but if you didn't go, he or she might not like you, so you go anyway. This person comes late to pick you up, and you don't say anything about waiting or ask why he or she didn't call or text you to let you know. He or she blows you off to go with some other friends and gives you an excuse later. When you are with this person, he or she makes you laugh and feel like you are special, but there are times he or she puts you on the back burner and you just continue to be okay with it. You may tell him or her that you don't like it or that it pisses you off, but you don't actually ever do anything about it. He or she keeps on being late or pushing boundaries. When this happens, you have already taught him or her that you can be treated this way. You might get mad or give him or her the silent treatment, but you never really do anything else. Then when it happens again, you may get mad again or go back to the silent treatment, but the relationship continues. When this happens, you also begin to treat him or her in certain ways and play get-back games or decide that you will hold out on sex or flirt with friends while you are together. You may even say things on a social media site and bag on him or her in some way or another, which starts another type of fight. Eventually there is more fighting in the relationship than anything else, but you don't want to break up because you think you love him or her or you just don't want to be alone—you are just not sure which.

There are other types of behaviors that may be happening and you are letting it slide. Some of these are borrowing money and never paying you back or getting together for sex only and no other type of relationship activity. He or she may tell you something like, "I had tickets for a show and dinner, but you were busy"; however, he or she only told you this after finding out you were busy. His or her actions and words do not match. There are also those who use people for other things, like drugs or the possibility of getting hired or promoted at work. When you allow people to treat you in a way of being used or in other ways that frustrate you and you tell yourself that it is okay, this gives them permission to continue to treat you this way. If you see yourself treating others this way, it may be time to look at how you treat yourself. Being treated this way and treating others this way is a direct reflection of your relationship with yourself. There are generally some similarities between how we treat ourselves and how others treat us.

Looking at your relationship to yourself is difficult. How can you see how you treat yourself? Here are some general ideas of ways to look into the relationship you have with yourself. Consider how many times you have told yourself you would lose weight or start working out. Your intentions are good, but the reality is you start the day thinking that you will do better, and by the time evening has come, you have gotten some wine to head home to sit in front of the tube and drink. You didn't do any type of exercise, and you drank more than you intended. It isn't the fact that you got the wine and sat in front of the tube; it is that you made a commitment with yourself and did not follow through with the commitment. What this says is that you respect yourself as much as the example above of the person that continues to blow you off. You are doing the same thing—telling yourself you will do something good for yourself and then not following through. Most of us would not treat others the way we treat ourselves. If you tell a friend that you will come over and help your friend change the oil in his or her car, then that is generally what you do. So why don't you do the same thing for you? You make excuses and allow these excuses to dictate what you do with your life. When these excuses take over your life, you become bored, depressed, anxious, overly stressed, fatigued, avoidant, withdrawn, and isolative. How can you expect others to treat you differently when this is how you treat yourself?

Have you ever had a time when someone appears in your life who treats you very well? He or she may respect your space, compliment you, listen to your problems, and support your decisions. As this person continued to respect you as a person, did you feel like something was wrong with him or her or with the relationship? Maybe you questioned his or her intentions or questioned him or her as a person. Maybe you even talked behind his or her back because somehow there had to be something wrong with him or her. Could it be possible that the problem was you and not feeling like you deserved to be treated this way so you took actions to muck up the relationship? You began pushing this person away or thinking he or she wanted something from you until eventually the person was not part of your life.

Generally when you find someone who treats you better than you treat yourself, there is a tendency is to push him or her away until the relationship ends because it feels too weird to be treated that way. What we think and feel about ourselves is usually what we get back from others. If you frequently make a commitment to get in shape or cut down on drinking alcohol but don't follow through, then you may have people in your life who tell you they will do something but it rarely happens. You may have people in your life that also make commitments to themselves and never follow through, but together you talk about all the reasons it didn't happen today and you excuse each other for what you didn't do. You also laugh it off and tell each other that it doesn't matter. This only enables both of you to stay stuck in the same place. Sometimes this is inadvertent and subtle so it goes unnoticed until you realize years down the road that you are having the same conversation you had years before and still not doing anything about it.

If you can take a look at your relationships and how these may be a reflection of your relationship with yourself, it may help you see where you can do some things to improve your life. If you have recently started a new relationship and this person is treating you differently, before you throw in the towel, you may want to look at whether it is because he or she is treating you better than you treat yourself, or is it because you want to be treated better? Use the information to improve your life. Work on treating yourself better, and your relationships with others will also improve.

Our lives tend to go in cycles, and many times we continue to do the same thing over and over expecting different results. You know this as the definition of insanity. Wanting things to be different and actually having things be different is up to you. When you begin to treat yourself like you treat your best friend, your life will change. When you talk to yourself the way you would talk to your best friend, your life will change. This has to start with you because no one else can change your life—only you can. Most of the time people treat themselves as if they were the mud on the bottom of their shoe that needs to be scraped off. Stop treating yourself as if you are the mud, and treat yourself as if you are the rain that washes off the mud. The mud is still there, but you wash it off and keep going. This mud no longer weighs you down. We make mistakes; that is part of life. We can also be accountable and learn to be human, an imperfect person.

Think about this. When you are getting ready to go out for an evening, what type of messages do you tell yourself? Do you criticize what you are wearing? How your hair looks? Do you wish you could look like someone else? Do you compare yourself to a friend or a celebrity? Do you tell yourself messages like, "My friends will all end up with someone to dance with, and I will end up alone"? Do you tell yourself you are dumb, or that you can't do anything right? All of these messages are messages that hurt your self-relationship, which will also hurt relationships you have with others—it is a vicious cycle. Now, you are not alone in this since we are all going through our own vicious cycle. The problem with this is that you can't fix anyone else. You can only fix you. Focusing on other people's problems is also a great way to avoid your own problems, which also hurts your self-relationship.

Most of us struggle in some way with relationships. There are many types of relationships, but trying to find the person to spend one's life with has become a challenge. Finding that special someone can improve life, but that person cannot fix your life. When someone is not happy with oneself and thinks that this special someone will make everything better, the relationship can be doomed from the beginning.

Mary was constantly dating and looking for someone to be with. She kept choosing people who were exactly opposite of what she said she was looking for. All of the dates were found through dating sites, except for the few times she would meet people in the grocery store or out shopping and would plan a date or give them her number. Each time she continued to find the same person over and over again. All of the characteristics were the same. The names were different, but the personality and problems were similar. She did not understand why she kept finding the same person with different names.

She would go out with this new person on a date and every time find all the different problems this person had. Each date there was a problem with the person and a reason not to like him. Each time it sounded very much the same. She wanted so badly to have someone special in her life, she was going against her own standards and dating people who did not fit what she said she was looking for in a relationship. At one point after about six weeks of dating someone, she moved in with a man she thought was the one; however, within two months the relationship ended. She was not happy and decided to move out. They had moved in together before finding out more about each other. They did not have the same family or spiritual beliefs. This short relationship was so volatile and abusive that after it ended, she swore off dating or looking for a relationship. This only lasted for about three months and she was once again dating people; however, after moving in with someone and having it go badly, she did not let herself get as close to these men as she had in the past. She would date someone for a while and then move on. She never tried to just be alone for a while to get to know herself. She could not even imagine not going out with someone. She finally decided she would write a list of fifty things she liked about herself, but she could only come up with nine things. She discovered how hard it was to think this way about herself, and she didn't like thinking about it. She kept working on it, though, to see if it would help her feel better about who she was.

This seems like something that would be easy to do, but most people who have tried this exercise have a difficult time coming up with reasons why they like themselves. Distractions tend to get in the way of dealing with yourself. Avoidant behavior also gets in the way of getting to know yourself. If you have not spent time with yourself lately, you may not know what a wonderful person you truly are. It may be time to look into your heart and discover something good about you. I challenge you to take a week and try this. Turn off the television and music, and spend time with yourself. This could be the start of a beautiful relationship with you. As you learn about who you are, what you value, and what matters most to you, you may also find that you have a lot to offer and that you deserve to treat yourself and be treated by others better. This can change the way you see yourself and give you a reason to stop self-destructive behavior and be nice to yourself.

If a week is too long, then take a day out of each of the next several weeks and spend time with just you. Go for walks without the earbuds in. Go to a coffee shop, get coffee or tea, and just sit and watch the activity going on around you. Write or journal and express something that has been on your mind for a while. Begin writing a list about what you like about yourself. If you enjoy drawing, get out a sketch pad and allow yourself to draw freely. There are many things you can do alone that will give you time to get to know you without any distractions, just you alone with your thoughts and emotions.

These thoughts and emotions can help you know what you value, why certain things upset you, and how to deal with yourself in a healthier way. You can find out that these thoughts and emotions are just that—thoughts and emotions. They may not need to be fixed or acted upon; maybe learning how these thoughts and emotions make you feel mentally, physically, and spiritually will let you know a better way to cope with them. These thoughts and emotions can be a problem, but only if you react to them without thinking through how you are responding or reacting. Generally if you are reacting to these thoughts and emotions without slowing down to determine the best way to proceed, the outcome can be worse than when the problem began.

It is amazing how many thoughts and emotions I used to react to. When I reacted, most of the time the reaction would make things worse. This is how it would go. Much of the time I would just go quiet and bottle everything up inside of me. I would not tell anyone how I was feeling, and after so many times of not talking about how I felt, I would explode on something that was so trivial I would end up hurting whomever I blew up at and myself because I would feel so bad for blowing up. I would say things I didn't mean and then feel bad for saying them. I have realized that most of these thoughts and emotions come and go as fast as I can blink my eyes. It is my job to decide which ones I need to talk about. I need to learn to own my emotions and be in control over the thoughts that I need to do something about.

Our thoughts and emotions are part of everyday life, and learning to have some type of control over what we do with these thoughts can feel freeing. Life is happening so fast that if you don't gain some control over how and when you react to life, you will end up in constant chaos, which will keep you in a whirlwind of drama, which will keep you stressed-out, anxious, depressed, and angry, which will keep you acting out with alcohol, drugs, sex, gambling, food, or many of the other behaviors used to avoid problems. Learning about yourself and how to deal with you and only you will help change this vicious cycle. Learning to own your thoughts, emotions, and actions can help you treat yourself better, and then you will be able to teach others how to treat you better. Learning to like yourself can be challenging because you have to go through the steps to do it, but it is so worthwhile.

Take some time to get to know you. Take the time to find out what makes you tick and how you can be in charge of your life.

Sometimes people say that "you can't teach an old dog a new trick," but this is just not so. As humans we have the ability to change our thoughts, be in control of our emotions, and find a little peace. This is possible if you take the time to get to know you and then take the time to be your friend.

Chapter 4

Mental Health Tip #4: Only bring from the
past that which will help you in the present.

This concept is similar to Buddha's teaching of not dwelling in the
past. Everyone has a past. Some of the events that have happened
may be hard to think about. However, these events can continue to
affect your life because there is so much energy and emotion about
the past event. Trying to stifle the energy, emotions, and memories
from these events can be self-defeating. Continuing to live in the
past and think about what you should have done will only increase
the energy of the emotion you felt during the event. This is what it
means to bring what you need from the past and let the rest of it be.
The negative energy and emotions that continue to affect your life
are from dwelling on a past that you cannot change. Continuing to
give the event time and energy will not ever change what happened;
it will only continue the hurt and pain you feel from this past event.

Many times we just try to block these events out; we use alcohol,
drugs, sex, TV, games, and any other distraction that will make
the event go away for a while. These events can cause feelings of
sadness, guilt, shame, embarrassment, anger, frustration, denial,
and numbness. Learning to let go of the past is easier said than

done. One of the reasons the past is hard to let go of is because we continually think about it, act out on it, and do the same thing over and over again, which feels just like the past. It has been said, that which is not learned from the past will introduce itself once again in the present. If you seem to continually have the same types of things happen to you, it is time to ask yourself why.

This is a hard question and may not be easy to answer. Looking at this concept in this way may help, so here goes. If you are continually going through similar events over and over again, it is time to ask yourself, "What am I doing to bring this into my life?" Something that is hard to conceptualize is that what we think about becomes what we do. Now it may not seem this way, but if you are continually thinking about your boss and how hard he or she is to work for, talking about how hard he or she is to work for with your coworkers, and getting aggravated whenever he or she comes and gives you something to do, which gives you more ammunition to think and talk about, eventually this will come around and bite you in the ass. This also keeps the aggravation high, which will keep you on high alert looking for every little thing he or she does to drive you crazy. It is like you become hypersensitive to your boss's actions and you are looking for the things that rub you the wrong way. This can be exhausting and a waste of time and energy. First, why would you want to give someone so much energy? Second, why would you give one person so much control over your thoughts? Is he or she really worth the amount of time and energy you are giving him or her?

Randy constantly complained about his boss. He would talk with his peers about how much he hated going to work because of his boss. He would instigate this talk with his coworkers and then feel validated because all of his coworkers felt the same way. He thought of his boss as if he was the enemy. One day his boss confronted him about all the things he was saying about him and how this was affecting the working environment, and then he fired Randy. Randy started telling his boss how much of this was his coworkers' fault and that they just didn't own up to what they were saying about the boss. He kept saying that if the boss only knew what some of his coworkers were saying about him, he would have fired them instead of him. He said that he wasn't the one that would start the conversations; he only agreed with his coworkers. Everything he said was about his coworkers; none of what he was saying was about his own actions. This was not the first time he had been let go. At another job he had gotten angry and said some things under his breath that his boss heard, and he was let go that night. He always had a problem with other people, and somehow it was always someone else's fault. His relationship with this boss was not good; he'd found reasons not to like him. He liked the job but found a reason to not like the boss. Both of these incidents have similarities. He struggled with his own actions and looked for someone to blame for problems in the job; it seemed he always decided it was the boss's fault.

So many times when something bad happens, we tend to look at everyone else's part in what happened, and we forget to look at our own. In the above example, Randy's actions in both jobs were similar. He talked bad about both bosses, which resulted in losing his job. When you look closer into this scenario, you may see that when he talked behind people's backs, it ended his jobs. It is important to connect his actions from both jobs to why he got fired. It was nobody else's fault but his. If he had worked on his communication with his boss and kept his thoughts about others to himself, he might have been able to keep a job he liked. Looking at his actions you can see that doing the same thing in both jobs gave him the same result—the loss of the job. In this story he continued to talk about others and got the same result from backstabbing. He will have to figure out how much he hurt himself by gossiping and saying things about someone else instead of using effective communication and dealing with what was really going on. His past continued to become his present because he continued to act in the same way and do the same thing, so he kept getting the same result.

Our past is a way for us to examine our life and see where we can change or where we have changed. An evaluation of our life is a way to determine if we are continuing to live in the past or moving forward with life. Our past can either become a gift of who we have become, or it can be a reminder of mistakes that have been made. These mistakes can either be something that continues to haunt us or something that helps us move forward. Reflecting on your day, your week, and your month can help you stay in tune with what is going on in your life. This can help you look at mistakes before you end up losing a friend or job.

Nobody likes the fact that a mistake has been made. Certainly the man who got fired does not like to think about how gossiping and talking about others behind their backs is what continued to make his life difficult. It was easier to blame others for getting fired. He is the only one who can change his actions, which will ultimately change his life. Does this mean he will never be fired again? No, it doesn't; it only means that he could be more aware of what his part of getting fired was. His actions are the only actions he can change. His boss may have been a hard boss to work for, but he cannot change his boss. He can only change the way he interacts with his boss and coworkers. Hopefully he can learn to communicate more effectively and stop doing the same thing over and over again and getting the same results.

Learning to accept our mistakes does not necessarily feel good. Most of the time, mistakes, especially if they are big ones, will feel like something that needs to be avoided. If you ask someone about something that has happened and this person feels embarrassed or shameful about their actions, usually the conversation will be averted or avoided. Sometimes these mistakes take on a cycle similar to grief and loss. One reason is that if you lose a job, you are experiencing a loss; if you lose a friend, then you also experience a loss. This loss is not like the death of someone close to you; however, these other types of events are still a type of loss in your life.

Divorce is a loss, and many people get stuck in the anger and never let go of what their partner did to them. There are a few problems with this thinking. The first one is that it takes two to tango, and a divorce is not just one person's fault. Second, if you are still angry at something that has already happened and the reason it happened, you have given this person too much control over your thoughts. You are allowing them to rent space in your head. If you have gone through a divorce, then maybe it is time to divorce the thoughts and let go of the anger, grudges, and reasons for the divorce. A divorce is not only on paper but in your thoughts, emotions, and actions.

When you look at the Kübler-Ross cycle-of-loss model, it looks like this. First comes the sadness and depression from the event. This depression is not like a clinical depression; it is a feeling of sadness, fatigue, exhaustion, low energy, agitation, tiredness, and avoidance. There is a tendency to shut out the world. Then there is denial; this is blaming everything and everybody else for what happened, not looking at your own actions or your part in what happened. Denial will let you feel like you are owed something because of what happened; there is also disbelief about what happened. Your view of what happened may be clouded because you will only look at what others did and not what you did. Next comes the anger, and this looks like however you show anger. It may be hitting or yelling at things, and it may be no talking, just closed body language and looks that come with daggers. The anger may also be more about the other person and what you would do to him or her if you were given the chance, fantasizing about the revenge that you would do. After the anger comes bargaining, and this is talking to anyone to see if things could be different or trying to make things look better than they really are. Sometimes it may be bargaining with your God or higher power. There is finally a point where you will feel acceptance about what happened. This is when you will be able to look at what you did and the result of your actions. You will be able to forgive those that you may have felt hurt you, and you will be able to forgive yourself for the mistake. It is the beginning of putting life back together.

I have worked with people after a divorce who could never get to this point. They wanted revenge so badly that they could never get past the anger and denial about their own actions. This loss cycle does not have to go in this order and you may spend more time in one stage than another, but as a general rule you will go through each of the stages—hopefully to get to the point that you have come to acceptance. If you still feel anger or resentment or want someone to suffer because of something that happened, you are stuck in the cycle of loss.

People go through the same cycle after they lose someone close to them or any big loss in life. Mistakes that are made that are big enough to change your life also merit this grief and loss cycle. This is because there has been a loss of something that has been a big part of your life, and because of a mistake it is no longer a part of your life. If you get stuck in one of the stages, this will keep you from moving forward in life. This can cause you to continue to make the same type of mistake over and over again until you either learn to let go of the past or something big happens to intervene in your life. The result of getting stuck in the loss cycle is problem after problem.

What are these big mistakes? Getting a DUI (driving while under the influence), sleeping with someone who is married or getting involved with someone while you are married, hurting someone you love either verbally or physically, gambling and losing money you don't have, being terminated from a job or quitting a job before you had something else lined up, damaging a car or something expensive of the person you blame, shopping and spending money you don't have—these are just a few of the mistakes we make as humans. These types of mistakes all cause loss in life because they are forever changing the way your life was. This doesn't mean the change is a bad thing; it just means you need to deal with it and let it go so you can move on.

Dealing with all of the mistakes we make as humans is not an easy task. Here are the facts: we all make mistakes, we have all done stupid things, and we all feel stupid when we have made a mistake. It is hard to own up to these mistakes, but the sooner you own your part and accept what happened, the sooner you can move forward with life, and who knows? The change may make life even better. If you are consumed by something that happened in your past, it may be time to learn to let it go. You cannot change the past. If you are living in the past and your thoughts are constantly about what should have, could have, or would have happened if only … it is time to let it go. Do the work and learn to forgive yourself and the other person or people involved and move on. You are making your present life miserable by focusing on and living in the past. It is over and cannot be changed.

Chapter 5

Mental Health Tip #5: When you learn to forgive yourself and others, your life will become less stressful, and small moments will feel like blessings.

Forgiveness is a hard topic, and this is why. When we have been wronged, there is a tendency to hold a grudge because the person that hurt us does not deserve to be forgiven. Most of us think that if you forgive this person, it lets him or her off the hook and he or she wins. Think about the last time you got into a big argument with your partner or someone that you are close to. Most of the time arguments happen because of a disagreement and then continue because of events from the past. These past events are the things that will tear a relationship apart. These past events will continue to haunt and hurt relationships until forgiveness happens.

John and Susan were a couple that was stuck in a cycle of hurt, blame, and guilt. He was injured at his job, so he was home all of the time. She worked full-time during the day in a customer service job. They had been together for about ten years and were married for four of those years. They had a young son, who was their pride and joy. Since John had been injured, he was at home, and he began drinking during the day most of the days of the week. He was also going out with buddies in the evenings because he felt cooped up at home all day long. Susan worked and came home and then took care of their son in the evening. Their relationship changed when John began spending money they didn't have, staying out late, and drinking more than he used to. This had been going on for about a year, and she was at her wit's end. They couldn't talk about anything without it turning into a fight. She didn't believe anything he told her anymore because his actions were saying something different. She started thinking that he was out with other women. The fight would begin and would end without getting resolved. They were on the verge of splitting. However, he did not want to separate and wanted to figure out how to stay together. She was tired of his lifestyle and ready to move on. They could not agree on anything.

Their relationship was full of mistrust and blaming each other in the relationship. She would focus on the time when he cheated. He would focus on someone he was seeing before they were together and continued to see when they got together. She was upset because he didn't tell her he kept seeing the other woman. He did break it off with this other woman shortly after, but about six months later he got together with her once more. His wife didn't believe that he ever quit seeing this other woman. She had never really trusted him from the beginning of their relationship, and this caused a lot of problems. He never really fully committed in the relationship, and her mistrust and his detachment became the cycle of the relationship. Whenever she would start talking about her mistrust, he would detach from the relationship and go out with his friends and drink too much, or just go out so he wouldn't have to have the same fight again. This was happening constantly, and both of them were tired.

Part of forgiving and letting go is realizing that you can never control what the other person is doing. The more she would try to control what he was doing, the more he would go out with his friends; and the more he went with his friends, the more her trust would decrease. She was becoming so focused on his life that she was forgetting about her own. He was hurting her constantly, and she was allowing his actions to rent space in her head and take away from what she could have been doing for her own life.

When we focus on someone else and his or her life and allow someone who has hurt us to continue to rent space in our head, this gives this person control over our thoughts, emotions, and actions. This may seem like a strange concept, but think about it this way. If you were in the store and someone cut in front of you in line, you may either tell him or her where the line starts or say something under your breath or something in between. This is not where the problem lies. How you let it affect your day is where the problem is. If the person that butted in front of you becomes the focus of your day and the focus of what you talk about, that person is renting space in your head. Your thoughts and actions revolve around this one incident that happened that morning. This gives this one person control, and he or she does not even know he or she has control.

This seems like a crazy idea, but think about the last time you were angry with someone who cut you off in traffic or brought you the wrong order. Did this incident make or break your day? Did this become the topic of discussion during the day? Did this change your mood or the way you treated other people during your day? The funny thing about this is that the person that may have cut you off has no idea that he or she is being cussed out or possibly ruined someone's day. We like to think that if someone did something like cut you off in traffic that somehow it had something to do with you. The fact is, what other people do has nothing to do with you personally; you just take it that way.

There is a tendency to take things personally, as if someone meant to do something bad to you. Even when you are in a fight with a friend or a family member, there is a tendency to take things personally and blow things out of proportion. Most people do not wake up in the morning and decide they are going to cut someone off in traffic or get in a wreck or deliver the wrong order or pick the same fight they have had with you over and over. If you take things as if someone is trying to do things to you intentionally, you will walk around with a chip on your shoulder and be angry most of the time or you will always be taking things personally, which will result in feelings of anxiousness, frustration, stress, and anger. Taking things personally will also make you do things you might not normally do, such as get revenge, say things you normally would not say, or talk to other people about the person you are pissed at, making sure that they know how bad that person is.

When it comes to a relationship, the hurt can run very deep. There are choices that will need to be made about whether both parties can move past the hurt, let go, and move on or whether the damage is too great to repair. In many couples's cases, the damage becomes too great to repair and eventually they split. Whether couples split or stay together, it is still necessary to let go and forgive so that the past does not affect the future.

Even if John and Susan split, she will have to work on her anger and feelings of being betrayed. She will need to work on what her part of the relationship problems was. It is important for both of them to look at whether they had quit talking to each other, stopped being intimate, or were not spending much time together even when they were home together. Each of them will have to forgive themselves for the things they did in the marriage and their anger toward each other. They will need to be able to be cordial and work on parenting their son even if they are not together.

Forgiveness is about you and allowing the past event to stop making the present moment about the past. The past is over. You can never go back in time and change what happened; you can only make a decision on how you react to the event. You can also decide how it will affect you moving forward. If you do not make a decision on how it affects you, the reality is that it will continue to affect you whenever there is an event or situation that is similar to the past. In the case of John and Susan, the past event kept coming up every time he would leave the house. It was never talked about or resolved. It just became a trigger to many, many fights, which ultimately could destroy the relationship. If you can learn to let go of the past and begin to heal, you will regain control over your life.

This does not let the other person off the hook; this lets you off the hook, and that is what forgiveness is all about. It is for you, not the person that has hurt you. When we forgive, it gives us space to allow other things into our life and let go of the clutter from the past, which takes away from our present life. Forgiveness is learning to let go and heal, so you can live in the present moment without letting all of the past cloud what is right now and have the ability to not personalize what others are doing around you. This is a very simple concept, but it is not easy; however, there is a tendency to make it more difficult than it needs to be. Allow yourself to forgive yourself and others; declutter your mind, let the past go, and live in the present moment. It is an amazing feeling.

Chapter 6

Mental Health Tip #6: When life gives you
lemons, take them—they are free.

I remember the day my granddaughter told me this, and I laughed and then thought about this saying. This is such a great concept because inevitably life is going to throw some lemons at us, so learning to change our perception about the lemons is genius. Our perception about our life is our perception and no one else's perception. This can be seen by asking several onlookers at an accident site what happened, and depending on their perception, the story will be told. There will be a general perception that will be talked about, which is the actual accident, and depending on their viewpoint, their emotions, the type of day they were having, and their thought processes will determine how they remember and discuss what happened.

There have been many studies done on memory and perception, especially from the viewpoint of witnesses who saw a crime take place. What happened at the crime scene and what our memory may have perceived can be significantly different. Imagine now if we take that into everyday life. At the end of a rough day, my perception may be that my boss is really hard on me, my husband doesn't care,

and I am alone trying to manage work, family, and homelife. So I walk around with a chip on my shoulder, thinking that I don't get anything back for all of the things I do for others, and by the end of the night I am curled up watching TV with food and alcohol so that I can drown out the day. This sounds like sour lemons, and I am drowning my problems instead of solving them.

The lemons in this case may not even be lemons, and if they are, do lemons have to be a bad thing? I can only take on the problems I know exist. I have to become aware of these problems before I can decide they exist. This means I may need to talk to other people and gain a better understanding or another perception of the problem. I can also talk to my boss about feeling overwhelmed and needing some help, which may leave me open to his or her scrutiny. If I am already worried about what my boss is thinking about my performance, then maybe before jumping to conclusions, I would be better off to talk about it professionally and hear what his or her thoughts actually are. Talking to my boss will actually calm down my negative, stressful thoughts that I want to drown out. These negative thoughts make me feel like I can't do anything right and cause me to want to go home and eat my emotions. When I follow this line of negative thinking, by the end of the night I will be more miserable than when the day started. If I talk to my boss, I may not like what I am told, but I won't be assuming what he or she is thinking. These conversations can be difficult, but the alternative seems worse. This is just one of the many conversations that probably need to happen.

By using my voice and talking about what is happening instead of bottling it up and assuming things that are not happening, I decreased my stress and found the information I needed by going to the person that could give me the information. I may not like the answers, but I have the information and can now do something about the problem. This will actually relieve stress and some of the pressure because I don't have to assume what my boss is thinking—now I know. As a general rule our assumptions are far worse than reality. We tend to make things big in our heads. So many times we are our worst enemy, or at least our thinking is.

There are ways to communicate that many times we don't really think about. If you were to have a conversation with your spouse, partner, boyfriend, or girlfriend, you may actually get the validation you are needing or at least find comfort. Letting your partner in on how you feel is part of being in a relationship. Now, can this get thrown back at you? Of course it can, but if you already feel alone, then what is the difference? You may as well express your feelings and ease some of those thoughts and resentments that are building up. Taking responsibility for your thoughts and emotions means that you may need to talk about them so you don't end up resenting others and making yourself a victim of what you think everyone else is doing to you. The fact is nobody does anything to you that you don't allow. So if you can learn to talk about how you are feeling, then you are taking responsibility for you and your problems and coming up with ways to solve these problems instead of living in the problem and complaining about it.

You are taking the lemons and doing something with them instead of sitting and stewing about what other people are doing to you. You will ease so much pressure by talking to the person that you are blaming or assuming something about. Here is a small example of what this can look like: Two people that work together continued to have conflict and get on each other's nerves during their shift. Mia took everything that Devon did personally, and it affected their working relationship. Mia didn't think that Devon took responsibility for anything that happened on their shift. Devon blamed anything and everyone else; she was nice to your face but would talk badly about her peers once they left the room. Talk about lemons. There are several ways to handle this situation, but only one way that will create a solution and resolution. Mia needed to talk to Devon, but would it even be worth it? The problem was that Mia didn't think it would go anywhere, so she kept it to herself for a long time and allowed her emotions and thoughts to get really resentful and vengeful. She started thinking of ways to get back at Devon; she would walk by and not make eye contact or not say anything to her, and would watch to see if she could catch her in a moment of doing something wrong. These tactics tied her up in knots, and her workday became consumed with Devon instead of her job and herself.

Mia finally went and talked to her supervisor, who told her a very good motto to live by. If you are avoiding someone by not making eye contact or thinking more about what he or she is doing than what you are doing, it is time to talk to the other person and clear the air. Mia knew it was time. She had to talk to Devon and at least clear up her side of the street; whatever Devon did with the information was none of her business. Mia asked Devon if they could talk and then began by telling her the frustrations and some of the incidents she had watched Devon blame on others. Devon was then able to tell Mia her side of the story and what had been happening. Mia listened to her frustrations and did not try to argue her side of the situation with Devon; she just listened, and when Devon was done talking, she asked Devon if they could come up with a plan to work together better. She suggested talking more often and coming up with a plan to get the teams working together. When this conversation was over, Mia felt better and had a better understanding of Devon as a person. This allowed Mia to have more compassion for her situation, and by opening up and talking, they were able to come up with strategies to work together.

First, acknowledging there were lemons and then doing something about the lemons helped create a stronger team. It also helped both of them resolve some of their differences. They still had differences but felt better after talking about them and working through them. Once Mia quit avoiding the situation and just went head-on into the problem, things got better. Mia's life got easier because she no longer had to avoid Devon. The team became stronger, and work once again became more enjoyable. Mia was no longer stressed over the fact that she had to go to work and avoid Devon; she could just go to work.

This can be a valuable lesson to learn. It is always easier to talk over problems; be honest and upfront, but also listen to the other person's side of the story. You will never be able to control someone else or make someone do something, but you can control your actions and the way you respond to others. In this instance Mia chose to be open and look for a resolution instead of a way to get back at Devon. These are choices we all have to make, but if you choose to be passive or aggressive, it will make the problem continue or make it worse. Learn to be assertive and talk about problems as they arise.

I have had times in my life where I wanted to be right and I wanted to win. When I would talk to the other person, I had an agenda of only getting my point across and making sure that the other person understood my point. This type of conversation becomes very one-sided. When you begin a conversation with this type of agenda, the conversation is already doomed. Neither party actually hears the other. The reason for this is because you are so busy coming up with what you will say next while the other party is talking that you do not hear each other. The conversation will usually become heated, and neither party understands what the other was trying to say. There are many assumptions that come from this type of communication that cause a lot of tension in a relationship. Once the conversation becomes heated, the communication is gone, and the conversation is really pointless. I look back on conversations like these and remember saying things I did not mean and getting so angry that I would throw something or walk away so pissed-off that I would binge-eat—as if that would fix the problem.

Problems are part of life, and learning to deal with the problems effectively is part of our life journey. I think about a saying often that Wayne Dyer says: "If you have the choice to be right or kind, take kind every time." I love this saying because it reminds me to remember that all of us are dealing with something in our lives. It is important to have empathy and compassion for others and be open to others' opinions and experiences. I am constantly reminded that I don't have all the answers and learning from others is a gift. This life journey takes strength, compassion, and the awareness that at any given time, our life can drastically change. To be present in life means that as these changes occur and problems arise, you learn to experience each moment even if the moment is giving you lemons. These lemons are a way to show you that you are living, you are alive, and not all of the life experience feels good. Not all of the life experience gives you lemonade. If you can think of each experience as a way to understand both the dark and the light, the happy and the sad, the angry and the compassionate, or the chaotic and the boring, you will see the beauty in life. The beauty comes from being present in each moment and experiencing these moments.

Taking life's lemons and accepting them for what they are is living life on life's terms, without fighting, controlling, or avoiding all of the experiences that life throws at all of us. It is understanding that thoughts and emotions ebb and flow. Once you can learn that emotions that do not feel good will pass and there is no need to avoid them, you will learn to accept those circumstances that come into your life (lemons). When life gives you lemons, take them; they are free to experience, teach you, and guide you.

Chapter 7

Mental Health Tip #7: Thoughts are just
thoughts. They only hurt if you react to
them ... remember, all thoughts will pass.

We think so many thoughts throughout the day that we don't even know what all of them are. Our brain has between 12,000 and 50,000 thoughts per day according to most research. Most of these thoughts are from our subconscious mind. Our subconscious mind thinks the same thoughts day after day. We are creatures of habit, and thoughts are no different. What is even more staggering is that about 80 percent of all thoughts are negative. Doesn't this make you wonder how we ever get through a day? These negative thoughts have been thought many times before and become a pattern of thoughts that you say about your life to yourself. These are the thoughts that sound like "I am so stupid," "I can't do anything right," "I don't have good luck," and "I just got screwed again." These thoughts can be self-destructive without you even knowing that they are or realizing that you're thinking them. I used to think that I didn't have any control over my thoughts, but I have found this is definitely not true.

There was a time that science thought the brain was fixed and at a certain age the brain was done growing and could not be changed.

This fed right into the thought of "you can't teach an old dog a new trick." The fact is you can teach your brain to think differently; this does take work, however. Negative thoughts can be tiring because these thoughts produce chemicals that deplete and weaken our physiology, which can create the feeling of being tired and stressed. When we think we "can't," "never," or "should have," or when we think complaints about ourself or someone else, these chemicals are produced, and we feel overwhelmed or stressed-out. If 80 percent of our thoughts are negative, think how much energy our physical body is using just to keep up with and deal with these negative thinking patterns.

Most everyone has met or knows someone who always has a positive outlook on life. There are also those who never seem to have a negative thought and are always happy. I used to think they must be quite fake and cover up a lot of their issues with a smile. The more I learn about the brain and our thoughts, the more I know this is not true. People who have the ability to remain positive most of the time are really quite lucky. Except that luck does not have a lot to do with it. It is more about brain chemistry and what someone focuses on. The chemicals their brains produce are the "feel good" chemicals that we all get when we exercise. We can also have this release of chemicals and feel good, for example, after sex or after we have done a random act of kindness for someone without feeling obligated to do it. These chemicals are powerful and can increase the energy of the physical body. Notice next time you are in a positive mood how much energy you have as compared to when you are in a negative mood. This is the mind and body connection, and it is a powerful connection.

Jared looked at the world as unfair, full of anger, and depressing. He felt like nothing ever went right for him, and the more he tried to accomplish a goal, the further behind he would get. He tried to go to school for a while, but he started hanging out with a group of peers that would smoke pot and drink every day. He felt as though this was the only time he felt accepted. He would talk to his friends about how bad the government is and how life is so unfair. He would talk about really heavy depressing things and about all the problems either in the world or with one of them. He would then go home and watch TV, which was full of violence. He really never had many positive thoughts about himself or the world. He never really thought about anything good and never thought about anything positive about himself.

This type of lifestyle makes it nearly impossible to have positive thoughts or have natural physical energy. He dropped out of school and lost his part-time job, which reinforced the thought that nothing ever went right for him. He blamed dropping out of school on his instructors and losing his job because of a coworker. There was no responsibility on his part; there was only negativity and blaming. How could he ever solve his problems and get out of this rut if it was always someone else's fault? He would complain about what his life was like but wouldn't change anything about his life. He would have to look at the way he was thinking and how negative he made his world, or he would never begin to change his world. If you are always negative about everything that is happening in your life, you may want to work on changing the way you view life.

We are responsible for our life, and our thoughts help create the world we live in. If you are living in a negative world, you may want to begin with your thinking by noticing what your thoughts are like. If you notice a lot of negativity in your thinking, you can change this. Your thoughts can change, but you have to become aware of these automatic thinking patterns. Once you are aware of these thoughts, you can begin to break this cycle of negative thinking patterns and change these thoughts.

Our thoughts influence the world in which we live. Our negative and positive thoughts are much more influential than you may think. A Japanese scientist, Dr. Emoto, investigated how thoughts influence our world by taping words onto two separate containers of distilled water. The words on one container were "You make me sick" and "I will kill you," and on the other container was "Love and appreciation." He froze the water and photographed the water over time while being frozen. The container with the loving words created snowflake-like patterns in the ice, and the container with the negative words created sharp images of disorder. This shows how much influence negative and positive thoughts or words have over our environment and our life. I was shocked as I watched this experiment and read his results. I understood how thoughts would influence my own life, but how these thoughts influenced the environment was not something I had ever really considered. This really made me think about how I think.

Changing your thoughts is a simple concept, but it is not easy. It takes consistency and dedication to decrease negative thoughts. One of the first things you can do is realize thoughts are just thoughts. Just because a thought comes in does not mean that you need to do anything with it. Matter-of-fact thoughts can float through our minds just like clouds in the sky, and if we think about thoughts in this way, it becomes easier to disengage and just allow the thoughts to roll on through.

Most of the thoughts we have roll through our minds without us even knowing we had that thought. With 12,000 to 50,000 thoughts per day, just think how many thoughts roll through our minds. Learn to use this concept to let those thoughts that upset you or create negativity roll through like clouds in the sky. Learn to notice the thoughts without giving these thoughts any power; this becomes an empowering process. These thoughts can only affect your life when you give them energy and react to the thought.

For instance, if you have had a hard day and you are in your car and somebody cuts you off and then slows down in front of you, your negative thought pattern may be something like this: "What a jerk, and now they are slowing down so I will just ride their ass and honk my horn." You keep as close as you can, and all of your focus is on the car in front of you. Meanwhile, you are feeling stressed and begin to yell at the driver even though he or she cannot hear you. You keep following, and then when the other driver gets into the right-hand turn lane, you pull up beside him or her and flip him or her off. He or she turns right, and you keep cussing because by now you are so focused on him or her that you have forgotten that you have a choice in your actions; you are actually increasing stress for yourself, and he or she is not even aware that you're pissed-off. You have worked yourself up to the point where now you need something to calm down, so you go to a bar, reach for a cigarette, or drive through the fast-food place to calm yourself, saying, "I deserve this now."

Once you get home, you tell your spouse or partner about the incident, and you find your stress level climbing again. Once you go to bed, all you think of are other ways that you could have made this person pay. You start thinking about the big bumper you would like to have on your car so you could just hit the people that cut you off. You try to sleep, but your thoughts are about what happened in the car, the rest of the day, the things you need to get done, the stuff at the house that needs to get done, and getting the oil changed in the car. The thoughts just go on and on, and it is hard to get to sleep. As these thoughts race, the incident with the car pops up again, and you can feel your heart beat a little faster and your hands clench with your jaw. Your thoughts turn to, "Why can't I just go to sleep?"

The energy that was given to this one incident has taken over your time and is in control of your thoughts, emotions, and behaviors. You may have eaten, drunk alcohol, or smoked many cigarettes because of this one incident. There is usually guilt about what you may have just eaten or how many cigarettes you just smoked. The guilt just makes the thoughts worse, and many times you will reach for more food or alcohol. This cycle takes over your evening, week, and month. This is how our thoughts drive us. The reality is we have control over these thoughts and could have taken a different approach right after getting cutoff. Being cutoff was just an event, but how you reacted to it was a choice. Being in charge of your thinking, your emotions, and your actions can change your whole life. It can also change your ability to sleep at night. Here is how it works.

You get cutoff, and instead of following really close and focusing on how the other driver just cut you off, you remind yourself that maybe the other person had a rough night or is heading to the hospital to see a loved one or any other possibility that could be happening. You ask yourself if you were having a bad day or just got bad news, would you be very aware of cutting someone off in traffic? Once you realize that someone cutting you off in traffic has nothing to do with you and everything to do with what is happening in the other person's life, it is easier to let it go. Learning to have compassion and empathy for others is very important.

We tend to personalize things that have nothing to do with us. Remember that other people are just living their lives and what they are doing has nothing to do with your life. Reminding yourself about other people's lives can get rid of a lot of thoughts that increase anxiety and stress. It is easy to personalize things that happen, but thinking that someone did an action on purpose just to piss you off is a little egotistical. Remember that none of us are that important.

You don't have that much importance that when you get cutoff in traffic, it was something that someone had planned to do to you. Letting someone else have this much control over your thoughts, moods, emotions, and actions actually gives him or her control over your life rather than you having control.

The thoughts you have guide your day. If you are frustrated with other people in your life and you focus on their actions, this will become your thoughts and your day. If you decide to focus on what you would like to accomplish during the day and keep this in your mind, this is what will guide your day. If you allow past events to be what you are constantly thinking about, these thoughts will guide your day. You are the sole creator of your day. If you have past events in your life that you struggle with and that continue to affect you, please go see a counselor or someone who can help you get through it. You do not need to carry the weight of the past through your whole life. I have worked with many adults who have kept events from their childhood secret out of fear that they would be judged or fear of being more hurt. Therapy is there to help you get through it; you do not have to be alone in your pain. Go see someone so that you can have the life you deserve.

Understanding how what you think can influence the outcome of your whole day can give you the information you need to stay out of the drama. This drama causes stress and makes life miserable. Once you learn that thoughts are just thoughts and you do not need to react to these thoughts, you will have more control over what you think and feel and how you act than you believe you do. Reacting to these thoughts only increases drama and affects life satisfaction.

Chapter 8

Mental Health Tip #8: When an emotion
comes, don't push it away, because the
more you push it away, the more it will
come back with a vengeance later.

Emotions are a fact of life. Humans are emotional beings, and as much as most of us hate to feel emotions like sadness, anxiety, despair, depression, annoyance, irritation, guilt, shame, or any of the other emotions that are not pleasant, these emotions are something that we all will continue to experience. Emotions are not going anywhere, so learning to deal with the intensity of the emotion is the key. Emotions are a part of life, and they are there to tell us that something is going on. Emotions tell us that something is bad or good, sad or happy, and depending on the intensity of the emotion, emotions can be extremely hard to handle.

If you are feeling down and upset, there is a reason you are feeling down. Henry was a successful businessman and ran a successful financial company. He did not like to talk about emotions and hadn't felt any emotions for a long time. He drank with his clients, but he would also drink when he got home from a long day. This eventually turned into a daily habit, and many times it would start in the middle of the day at business lunches. He also had a fair amount of physical pain from an old sports injury. He would take his painkillers most nights, but this eventually turned into several times a day and then more than that. He would drink and use his medications for stress, pain, emotional pain, and anger. If a deal went bad, he would drink and go numb. If he got in a fight with his wife, he would go out, take pain medications, have a drink, and stay numb. When he would come home, she would be asleep and he would go to bed, get up early, and leave for work. By the time they would talk again, the problem was forgotten—at least by him.

He continued to numb his emotions using prescription pills and alcohol until he got pulled over by the police and got a DUI. Getting a DUI can be the wake-up call for many people. It is an intervention that can help people who have been asleep from their emotions for most of their lives. For Henry this was a wake-up call. He started realizing how much he was using and how long it had been since he was drug or alcohol free. He really did not feel normal unless he had taken his pills. He had been avoiding his emotions for so long he did not know what it felt like to feel. He thought that throughout his life, he did not avoid anything; he dove headfirst into everything.

He remembered during childhood that he often tried to keep up with his sister, who never did anything wrong. He always felt like he was never good enough. He thought his dad was critical of everything he did, and so he learned to just do things and not worry about anyone else. He had a perception of how his sister was treated and felt resentment toward her. He was not close to his family. He had decided that success and making money was his key focus. His career and money were what kept him going. He had never really thought about his emotions and what he was feeling at any given time because mostly he was just focused on making money and avoiding feeling like he felt when he was younger.

This is definitely not an unusual story; it seems to be a common theme in so many adult lives. In my own life, dealing with emotions was never really part of life. I grew up with the sayings "Big girls don't cry" and "If you cry I will give you something to cry about." These are very common themes that have been said to so many. When these are the things that are said every day to you as a child, you begin to believe that crying, being sad, or being down or upset are not good things, so you learn to hide these emotions and put on a happy face even though inside you may not feel that way.

This decreases our ability to deal with intense emotions. Dealing with emotions is sometimes referred to as emotional intelligence; if people are using alcohol, drugs, sex, food, or other fixes to deal with emotions, then their emotional intelligence score is probably fairly low. If we are not sure how to handle intense emotions, we tend to use fast fixes to help out. The fixes—like alcohol, drugs, food, sex, shopping, work, gambling, TV, or social media—numb the emotions. Constant numbing of emotions will result in some severe explosions, which can look like angry outbursts, overeating or binge eating, sleeplessness, drinking and doing something you would normally never do, isolating and ignoring family and friends, working fourteen or more hours every day, using pornography and other sexual behaviors to feel better, gambling, or watching excessive amounts of TV; there are so many other behaviors as well that are used to avoid dealing with life and emotions.

Emotional intelligence is measured based on how well a person understands and deals with his or her emotions, how well a person handles other people's emotions, how a person relates to society, an individual's relationship with himself or herself, and how an individual deals with adversity. These can be assessed to determine an individual's ability to cope and handle his or her emotions, as well as areas that he or she can improve upon. What all of this does is help someone know his or her ability to handle emotions and learn other ways to deal with them without turning to unhealthy coping patterns.

Emotions can be like either a ticking time bomb or a cloud drifting in the sky. If you choose to avoid the emotion and cover it up, the emotion will come back time and time again and eventually lead to panic attacks, constant depressed moods, feeling angry all of the time, or just being numb all of the time. None of these are good options because eventually the emotion will seep out, and what we do then is usually something that we later wish we could take back. Anger outbursts are a good example of this. If you keep your emotions inside and do not talk about what is bothering you, eventually you will blow up. Usually the blow-up is about something small, which is usually just the tip of the iceberg. Since you blew up, everything that had been bothering you has now had a little relief (you blew off some steam); however, you still don't deal with what is really bothering you, and so the blow-up will happen again and again. It is just a matter of when the pressure builds once again and you blow up again.

When you deal with your emotions, it feels a bit like watching a cloud in the sky. This may seem like a strange metaphor, but here is why. Emotions come and go; we have emotions all day long. Some of the emotions we do not even consider; we just keep moving without realizing that the emotion just moved through us. Other emotions are intense and can create a lot of physical symptoms. These are generally what we react to. If you are feeling anxious, then you may have racing thoughts, a nervous stomach, or tense muscles, and feel sweaty. Trying to calm this emotion down with alcohol may seem like a good answer, but it does not help resolve the reason the emotion is there in the first place; it just covers up the symptoms. If you become aware of your emotions and can allow them to help guide you, it would look like this. When the anxiousness hits, recognize first that the feeling is anxiousness, take a look at why you might be feeling anxious, and then look for a resolution to the problem that brought on the anxiousness, finally finding a healthy way to calm down the symptoms of anxiousness, such as talking to someone, writing, listening to music, or drawing. If the anxiety comes on when you don't tell people "no" and you are always saying "yes" to their requests even though you don't have time or it is interfering with your own life, then when you start being aware of the anxious feelings in that moment, you may be able to start saying "no" and taking better care of yourself instead of adding pressure to your life until you blow up at someone who is not really part of the problem.

Emotions come with a lot of energy, and when an emotion like frustration, worry, anger, or jealousy comes, it can make you feel like you are going to lose it. This type of energy can be expended by movement. Getting the body moving can help decrease the physical symptoms of the emotion. Movement also helps clear your head of all the crazy thoughts that come with the emotion. These thoughts are the ones that assume things about others, put plots together to get back at someone else, go back in time to all of the bad things someone has done to you, and tell you that you don't deserve better. In other words, these thoughts are negative and will increase the energy of the emotion, which will increase the likelihood of doing something stupid like slashing your boyfriend's tires because you found out he was flirting with another girl.

Sometimes it may feel like slashing tires will make you feel better than getting out and running or biking to get rid of this energy, but whether you slash tires or run, this does not change what the other person did that may have hurt you. Slashing tires will result in a lot more drama and heartache in the end. So you have choices. If you can slow down by moving your body and clearing your head, you will make better choices and learn to talk about what is upsetting you instead of just blowing up. This is a way to take care of yourself in these highly emotional times. This self-care is part of learning to regulate emotions. Understanding and knowing how to deal with your intense emotions can help you become less reactive and keep you from texting someone a hundred times a day because of an argument or disagreement.

So many of us are looking for that special someone to spend our life with. Most of our stories are similar. Find someone who could be the one, move too fast or too slow, trust this person and find out you can't trust him or her, lose this person, and have a breakdown doing things that are not what you normally do. Anytime another person is involved, it can make it hard to regulate how intense your emotions are and how you react to certain situations. Learning to regulate your emotions and your reactions will improve your life and your relationships.

Kristin had been single off and on throughout her life. She was ready for a long-term relationship. She was dating a little bit and had found a man that she thought was someone she could spend her life with. They had a lot in common and spent a great deal of time together. They lived a few hours away from each other, so they would talk nightly on the phone and see each other most weekends. They had been seeing each other for about three months. The last weekend they were together, she talked about making the relationship more permanent, hoping that he was thinking the same thing. He smiled and gave her a big hug but never really gave her an answer. She assumed the hug was the answer.

When she called him on Monday night, it went to voice mail, and she figured he would call her back. She did not hear from him. She texted him the next day and still received no answer. She started texting him constantly, asking him to call her and let her know that he was okay. She did not get an answer. She continued to text him, still without any word from him. She looked on a social media site page to see if anything had happened and saw he had posted a picture, so she knew he wasn't hurt. By Wednesday she was in a panic and was considering driving to his house to see what had happened. She started searching her mind for what had happened and could not think of anything. Thursday night she got in her car and drove to his house but did not go to the door; she just sat outside, watching to see if she could see what was happening. She started thinking that he had someone else or maybe he wasn't even single in the first place. She let her mind wander and began thinking about what she could do to his car. She started thinking about his job and how she could tell people what a jerk he was. She sat there for a long time trying to see anything that would validate the reason he was not talking to her. She eventually left and drove home. She couldn't believe that she let someone in and believed that he was the one. She was angry, hurt, and on the verge of doing something really stupid. She texted him constantly that night telling him things like "I will cut your balls off," "You are the biggest f**n ass I have ever known," and "I am going to let everyone know what you are." These texts went on and on.

The next morning she asked herself the question, "Did all of that change the outcome?" She seemed to come back to the present moment, and her anger seemed to subside. She began to see how crazy she felt and how what she had been doing this week was so unlike her. She felt disappointment in herself and how she allowed someone else to have control over her emotions and her actions. She had to find a way to make the pain stop and calm down without giving him the power she had just given him. When she began to deal with the emotions of hurt, embarrassment, and now guilt for acting so out of sorts, she started looking at ways to take care of herself or self-care. She began writing and exercising to help her get control of her emotions. She began to understand and deal with how she was feeling. She started walking and reflecting about herself and what the experience may have meant for her. In time she could work on letting go of the grudge and forgiving him for treating her badly and herself for acting out and ultimately treating herself badly too.

He definitely did not treat her well, and he could have at least given her something to let her know why he was breaking it off or it wasn't what he was looking for. She may never know what his reasons were for what he did; however, she will always know what she did and how she acted. Being able to get up in the morning without regret is important. Most of the time, what other people do is about them and not about you. If you can remember this the next time someone does something and you get hurt, it will help keep you from getting into the crazy revengeful thoughts and actions. Learning to let things go and making sure that your side of the street is clean is ultimately what matters. This takes being able to deal with your emotions effectively.

Forgiveness can be a hard thing to do, but in the end forgiving those who have caused hurt will ultimately set you free. Emotions over time will decrease, and time will heal. Doing self-care will help you not do hurtful things back to someone because he or she hurt you. Revenge may feel good in the moment, but in the long run you will feel worse for doing it. In the above story, what he did was not okay. What she had to deal with was very difficult because it made her second-guess everything she thought she knew. It made her mistrust her own judgment, and it made her lose trust in others, which will keep her from the next person who comes along that may be the perfect person.

Emotions are inevitable and are part of the human experience. Learn to listen to the emotion, name it, and be aware of why it is happening. Once you are more aware of the emotions you experience on a daily basis, you will begin to know and understand why you are feeling certain emotions and how to deal with the emotion. Most of the time emotions ebb and flow just like life, and there is no need to fix them or try to make them go away. Just acknowledge the emotions and work on taking care of yourself when they become more intense because of an event or situation.

If you have been numb for a long time, it may be difficult to get in touch with any emotions. When you constantly numb your emotion, you forget what it is like to feel anything. You get used to numbing away or running from the emotion. Sometimes you may use social media or TV to take your mind off your emotion. There are times when the emotion is too much, and so it feels like the only option is to go numb. Numbness, however, is also an emotion; it serves a purpose and sometimes allows us time to digest what has happened and how to deal with it. Being numb for a long period of time, however, is not healthy.

After a devastating loss, you may use numbness as a way to cope with feelings of grief. After my son died, I went numb for a few years. I couldn't feel anything. I actually couldn't do anything either. I was stuck, and I was not even aware of it until I started feeling the loss. In those couple of years after he died, I got divorced, I lost my job, my stepdad died, my dog that was always at my side died, and then my best friend died. I never felt any of this. I went to funeral after funeral. I had my dog cremated and put him on a shelf. I kept waking up, going to work, helping others with their problems, going home, taking care of my grandkids, and going to bed. I had basically shut down my own emotional reactions and how I felt about all of the loss or any part of life and just kept focusing on others. I didn't taste food, nor was I interested in food. I ate because I needed to, not because I wanted to. I didn't laugh, cry, or feel anger. I didn't feel anything; I didn't enjoy anything. I had lost interest in so many of the things I used to love to do.

One day I felt the need to run or get in my car and just drive; I just needed to be anywhere but where I was. I was exhausted and just wished things would change, but I could not figure out how to make things change. I decided it was time to take a road trip to the beach. I decided that I would take my dog that I had put on the shelf to his favorite beach and let his ashes go. So that Saturday I left at about five o'clock in the morning to head to the beach that he loved to go to. I arrived at this beach around eleven o'clock, and it was a beautiful day. There were lots of dogs and dog owners at the beach. They were throwing sticks and balls, and the dogs were wagging their tails, going to get the ball, and bringing it back. I loaded George (my dog) into my beach bag and found a spot where I was away from other dogs and their owners. I sat and watched all of the dogs and began to notice how happy they all seemed.

I started thinking about George and how much I missed him. I started thinking about the last time we were at this beach and how many people came up to see him. You see, he was a 228-pound English Mastiff, and people always stopped us or wanted to pet him; he loved it. He thought he was a lapdog. I missed him. I started thinking of how much I missed my son and the last time we were at the beach. I missed his laugh, his smile, how he could make friends no matter where he was. He could walk into a grocery store and walk out with a phone number and a new friend. I missed him so much. I started thinking about my son and my dog being together, and this brought a smile to my face. I started to realize that I had tears running down my face as I sat and reminisced. I sat there with George in a can next to me and let my thoughts take me away. I don't remember how long I sat there, but there was a moment that I knew it was time to let George go, so I opened up the can and let his ashes go. I spread them around in the sand next to some rocks overlooking the water. He would have loved the spot. In that moment I felt things that I had not felt in a long time. I felt sad and peaceful at the same time. This was a healing moment that allowed me to let go of some of the pain I had been hanging on to. There had been so much pain over the last five years that I just shut down; going numb was how I dealt with all of the loss. Letting George go helped me heal a little part of what I had been trying so hard to keep away. Once again George helped me, just like he did when he was alive.

This was the beginning of the healing for me, and I am still working on healing through the loss. I have come to terms with my stepdad, my job, the divorce, George, and my best friend. I still struggle with my son; it is a loss that has left a hole in my heart that is always there. Memories, pictures, and talking about him do help. Nothing will ever change what has happened; the only thing that I can change is how I choose to respond to his death. I decided I wanted to honor his memory and stop existing and start living because that was how he lived. He loved life and did more in his short life than many do in their entire lifetime.

We all have things that have happened in our life that can disrupt everything about our life. Our response to these events is our choice. I know being numb was a way to get through all of it, but it was not how I want to choose to live. Slowly but surely I am once again feeling not only emotions like sadness, frustration, anxiousness, and anger but also emotions like peace, joy, happiness, and gratitude. I have also started to again enjoy the taste of food, which is progress.

Chapter 9

Mental Health Tip #9: It is okay to ask for help.

This mental health tip can be one of the hardest. One reason for this is that none of us like to admit we may need some help or that we can't do something on our own. I have lived my life this way. I was brought up in a family where my parents would buy the things I needed and I would buy the things I wanted. This meant that I had to learn to work and make money very early. I would babysit any chance I had, and at fourteen years of age, I lied on an application to get a job. I started working at a place called Grand Central, which in the seventies would have been comparable to the Wal-Mart of today. I was a cashier and would help stock shelves and do inventory. I probably worked about twenty hours a week, but this meant that most Friday nights and Saturdays I was working. I remember being envious of my friends who were heading to the mall on Saturday or the Friday night football game and the dance afterward. However, I liked making money and being able to buy some things I wanted. I began learning that working and making money was how I could get what I wanted even though I was missing out on some things.

I enjoyed the job and made some friends there too. I also found my first boyfriend there. We worked a lot of the same shifts. When we worked together, we would take our breaks at the same time if we could or call over the loudspeaker to pick up a certain line so we could talk for a minute. We were together for about two months, and then he found out that I had lied about my age. He thought I was sixteen, and I was really a few months from turning fifteen. I quit working there not too long after that, and I never heard from him again. I never talked about this with anyone or admitted that I was hurt after he broke up with me. I kept it all inside. As a result I quit my job and wrote the whole thing off as "I am not good enough."

My family is a very close family, and as I became an adult and had kids of my own, we would get together and do things for my grandparents. We would go mow their lawn and do yard work, and then once we were done, we would sit on their deck and eat homemade popsicles my grandma had made. Most of my life when we would do things as a family, it would be around some type of work. So, what does this have to do with asking for help?

I learned very young that working hard was the cure for most everything. Doing house chores and yard work from early on was how we would spend our Saturdays. I learned that crying was not a good option, and being too excited was not good either. I grew up with a younger and an older brother, so keeping up with them seemed to get better results than being a girl. This also meant that you did things by yourself without asking for help. If I couldn't figure something out, I would fake it and say I did it. I would also say that I understood something when I really did not. I would do this at school with assignments or with a game I was playing with my friends. I never would say that I didn't understand something because that would make me look like I was weak, and weakness in my family was not really an option, or at least that was how I perceived it. If I admitted I didn't understand, it also meant that again, I was not good enough. That was just not going to happen.

As I took this into my adult life, I was unable to say, "I don't know the answer to that'" or "I am not sure how to do that." This was in all parts of my life. I remember when my son was about two, and he was biting, hitting, and kicking other kids in day care. The day care teacher told me some ways to help him, and I would say things like, "I have already tried that" or "I already do that." I wasn't open to any suggestions and wanted people to know that I knew what I was doing even though I didn't. When I sold real estate, I would act like I knew what I was doing, not asking for suggestions from the people who had been selling for a long time. I really made my first few years of real estate harder than they needed to be. I would do the monthly bills and would juggle money from one place to another. I spent way beyond my means, but I could never admit that I couldn't have or do something; I would figure out how to make it work, even though it was putting me further and further into a hole. I could not admit I made a mistake or that it was my fault for our financial trouble; I would find something to blame it on and make excuses about my financial problems. Asking for help was not an option, and if I admitted I didn't know something, this meant I was not good enough. What a double bind I had myself in.

When I look back at that time in my life, I realize how much stress and pressure I had put on myself. It was really difficult to try to keep up an image of knowing everything and being perfect at everything I did. I thought I was good at keeping up this image, but the truth was that the only person who didn't know I was making mistakes was me. I kept up a certain image or appearance and didn't want anyone to know that inside I felt inadequate and unsure of myself. I had a good friend tell me once that I was sending out the representative when I was around other people, but when I was alone I was just me.

One day this really hit me and I began to cry. I didn't just cry; I sobbed for most of the day. I couldn't stop. I started writing all of the things down that were wrong with my life. I started writing about all the lies I was living and how I just wanted to be myself whether I was by myself or with other people. I started talking to a counselor and asking what I could do to change my life. As I started doing some of the assignments, I began to realize how hard I had been on myself. I started writing about how I wanted to change my life and the things I was going to do. I started asking for forgiveness and telling God, or the Source or whatever you would like to call your higher power, that I wanted and needed help. I made a commitment to myself and God that I was going to change.

From that day forward, I changed. I started admitting to my mistakes; I stopped blaming anybody else for my problems. I started cleaning up my life, and it felt really good. It felt good not to bring out the representative. It felt good to just be myself. It felt good to say, "I don't know the answer to that," instead of, "It is because of this person that this happened," using the blame game to hide my own inadequacies and problems. I was able to say, "It is my fault," or "Oops, I made a mistake." Once I admitted to the mistake or that I didn't already know the answer, I could then begin either finding out or solving the problem, and this felt a lot better. All of a sudden my finances changed and I was in control of my money and where I was spending it. I was in charge of my life, mistakes and all.

When you try to portray an image or be something or someone that you aren't, there is a price to pay. The price is not being true to who you are and ultimately going against what you believe, living for others and what you think they expect from you. You make assumptions about what people think about you and then react to these assumptions. You create drama and problems that keep the focus off yourself. You try to look perfect and create an image that is very hard for others to live up to. When you make yourself something you are not, eventually the facade will unravel and life will fall apart. Living for others creates an enormous amount of pressure and stress. It creates a life of doubt and assumptions. It creates a life of untruths and cover-ups.

Asking for help is the beginning. Asking for help and knowing that we are all humans and humans make mistakes is freeing. Learning that mistakes are inevitable and admitting to these mistakes was the best thing I ever did for myself. Asking for help can make you feel very vulnerable, and being vulnerable is not a good feeling. When we feel vulnerable, it feels as if everything is exposed and that being hurt is inevitable. I compare being vulnerable to an open wound; if someone were to pour salt in your open wound, it would hurt more than anyone could bear. Being vulnerable does not make you more open to being hurt; it just makes it so that you don't have to hide or justify your life. Being vulnerable allows you to be real, honest, and open to the world around you. Being vulnerable allows you to be yourself. You don't have to hide your mistakes, you don't have to justify or rationalize the reason you do things, and you don't have to blame others and feel guilty later; you just have to work on being you, plain and simple. Being vulnerable allows growth, being vulnerable allows for mistakes, and being vulnerable allows you to love and be compassionate toward others. You won't judge or criticize others for their mistakes because realizing that we all make mistakes is part of the beauty. This brings empathy and compassion into your life. This compassion is not only toward others but also toward yourself.

Asking for help can feel like a weakness, but it is actually a strength. This is why. Asking for help or even admitting that help is desired allows other people to be part of the process. This allows other people to use their strengths, gifts, and talents to assist you. It was explained to me like this. Every time I try to do everything on my own and never allow anyone to help me, I take from others. This is because when I do it all, this never allows others to discover or learn for themselves. Here is an example: I was selling real estate and teaching several classes at the local gym. I would get home around dinnertime and then start the laundry, dinner, and homework with the kids. As the kids got older, I continued to do it all, even though my son, who was twelve at the time, wanted to do his own laundry and learn to cook. If I taught him to do this, he might not need his mom as much, so I kept control and would always tell him I would do it. This control and need to be needed kept him from growing and learning to be more self-sufficient. As parents, isn't that what we are trying to get our kids to do?

I was so backward in the way I thought. After I had this huge self-reflection and epiphany, I started showing him how to do his laundry and cook eggs to start. He began keeping up with his laundry and actually did his laundry better than I ever did. He also began cooking and found out that he really liked to cook. This took pressure off me and allowed me to take a different role with my son. I also let go of trying to keep my daughter's hair the way I wanted it; I let her do her hair the way she wanted it. She learned to do her hair by herself and then asked for help if she needed it. What a concept! As I let go of all the control and needing to do it all on my own, my kids took pride in learning and doing things. They asked for help or validation and confirmation with, "How did I do?" which allowed me to still be a part and either give hugs and high fives or help out. I was still needed, but instead of my needing to be needed, it was more about feeling valued for passing on information and watching them succeed. They were learning to ask for help, take care of things for themselves, and gain confidence.

Milly was a woman who was struggling with leaving her husband and nine-year-old daughter for a few weeks. She was worried because her daughter did so many activities after school and she went to the school to help out twice a week; she didn't believe her husband could do this and take care of the house, cooking, getting groceries, cleaning, doing the laundry, and taking care of the dog and bird. She really wanted to go with some friends on an excursion but wasn't sure that she could go and not come back to a big mess. She didn't think her family would survive. She was also worried about what would happen if they did get along without her. If they could get along without her, then it would never be done the way she would do it. She started to realize that if they could get along without her, it might mean that they were actually okay without her. She began to realize that she didn't want them to make it without her because that would mean they didn't really need her. Once she realized this, she could work on what was really going on and learn that she would always be needed; she could let go of some of the control and lean on others to help her.

Asking for help has a ripple effect. Letting go of so much control and trusting others to help out or handle certain situations gives them the feeling of being valued, it builds confidence, and it gives you the opportunity to help others grow. Letting go is the first step. Once you do this and come to terms with the uncomfortable feeling of not being in control, you may find that you have more control. Once you try asking for help and begin to let go of the perceived control, you will wonder why you didn't do this sooner. It is okay to ask for help. It is better than okay, I think. As you try it, you will find it refreshing.

Chapter 10

Mental Health Tip #10: Movement is one
of the keys to feeling good about life.

There are many times when sitting on the couch and vegging out
to the TV seems like the best idea. Life can become overwhelming.
Feeling overwhelmed can zap all of your energy, and sitting on the
couch with food and a drink while watching something on the tube
is all the energy you may have. Sometimes this is good to do; it can
give your body and your mind a rest, which can help you carry on.
However, if you are doing this all of the time, it can become very
self-destructive and harmful. Notice that I said sometimes sitting
and vegging out to the tube can be helpful, but if this is happening
most of the time, it is not helpful. It probably means that you are
avoiding life or you are bored in life.

If watching TV, eating copious amounts of food, drinking
alcohol or soda, and not moving is the way you are dealing with
this stressful life, you are doing yourself more harm than good.
Here is why. There is no doubt that life has become increasingly
more stressful. Life is also happening at a much faster pace, which
means that we expect things to happen faster and results should
be quicker, and as for patience—well, it is being thrown out the

window. Everything you do with technology is instant, which makes it seem that everything else should be instant too. The problem is that finances, weight loss or gain, raising kids, creating a healthy relationship, or stopping an addiction are more like a marathon than a sprint. What I mean is that these are lifelong journeys. When these types of life goals or events don't happen in, say, a week or maybe even a month, there is a tendency to give up and sit on the couch and veg out.

If weight loss is the goal, sitting on the couch with food and alcohol will never help you reach the weight goal you are striving for. If finding a healthy relationship is your goal, you will never find that special someone sitting on your couch. What you will find if you are sitting vegging out, eating, and drinking is negative thoughts, numb or negative emotions, an unhealthy body, and a pretty big pity party that can last for months if not years. You will not find the relationship you want, you will not lose or gain the weight you want, and you definitely will not find the job you want if sitting at home and watching movies or TV is your life.

This pity party becomes a way of life, and it can look like this. Get up in the morning wishing you could stay in bed, get ready for the day, listen to the news, get angry about what is happening in politics or a headline that really pisses you off, head off to work in a bad mood and yell at the car in front of you that is going too slow, yell at someone for cutting you off, get to work and complain to anyone who will listen about the news you saw, blame everything that happens to you on politics, traffic, or some other aggravation in your life, and the day continues in this same manner. On your way home, maybe you stop and get fast food because cooking is not an option; once you get home, you turn the TV on and eat, drink, and go numb. Of course there may be family to deal with or things the family is doing, which only puts on more stress and pressure, partly because when your pattern is interrupted by something out of the normal, it becomes frustrating and another reason to be upset. Over time this behavior becomes more of a habit and a pattern that can be very difficult to break. If you are a big sports fan and watch every sport that is on or you watch a certain talk show without fail, the moment that you can't watch your show, you automatically become frustrated that something is interfering with your plan. Even if you can record these shows but you have a plan to watch them at a certain time, you may still get frustrated if your plan is interrupted. Think about a time when your daily routine was interrupted—how did you react?

When you react to life and all of the pressures that life brings by numbing or vegging out, your brain becomes accustomed to handling all pressure and stress in the same way. Anytime you feel stress, anxiety, overwhelm, depression, anger, and so on, your brain will tell you that TV, drinking, and food is what will make things feel better. This becomes an automatic reaction or autopilot. Pretty soon you don't even realize that this behavior is self-destructive and is hurting you. Your brain and your body are accustomed to numbing out, which can make change very difficult because you have trained yourself to react to stress, anger, depression, anxiety, guilt, and life in this way. Beginning to retrain the brain to think differently is a difficult task, but it can be done. There are many coping skills that you may be using daily, but many times these coping skills become destructive.

Movement is the key to getting through many of the negative aspects of life. When you sit in negativity, it only creates more negativity, which grows and grows. Once this becomes a habit, it then becomes stagnation. Have you ever had a time in your life where life is the same day after day? Similar to the movie Groundhog Day. The same day over and over. This is being stagnant. Living day after day and looking forward to getting home to turn on the TV, reach for a cold beer, and throw food in the microwave is not living. There are many times when this is an option or a way to renew or reenergize, but when it becomes the way of life, it can create a negative existence.

The reason that movement works is because when we are physically active, it increases the endorphins and serotonin levels in our brain, which has been shown to improve moods. This can help you get out of the pity party state and stop focusing on negative things. Movement will give you exactly what you are trying to get from TV, food, and alcohol, but you will feel better afterward. You will have a better outlook on life, you will not have any guilt and shame about your actions, you will not wake up in the morning feeling bloated or sick, and you will be improving not only your mental health but also your physical health. Using movement as a coping skill may seem like it would be too much to do when you feel overwhelmed or fatigued, but if you can spend even ten minutes going for a brisk walk, you will reap the benefits.

I have worked with many clients over the years and have heard every excuse in the book. I have been physically active most of my life, but in 2004 when I started getting sick a lot, my physical activity slowed down. I went to several different doctors and kept being told the same thing: they could not find anything wrong. By 2006 I stopped going to the doctors and just started taking a lot of Ibuprofen to get through the day. I was still working out a few times a week and walking at least three times per week. I knew this would help my moods, and doing this didn't make the pain worse or better. I figured I might as well move since either way I experienced pain.

I kept this going for a few years, and then August 2008 my son died in a fatal car accident, and I fell apart. I went numb to everything except physical pain. I did not know how to handle any part of life, and so by November 2008, I went back to a doctor, who told me my neck was degenerating and I had spinal spondylosis. He told me I needed surgery and it wasn't something that could wait. He gave me some names of doctors who did this type of surgery and a couple prescriptions for pain, and I left his office knowing I wasn't going to do any surgery on my neck but I would take the prescriptions.

After my son died, I found myself single again, and I threw myself into work. I avoided everything. I was disconnected and disengaged; I could not get my head around the fact that my son had just died, so avoiding was what I did. I ate food but could not taste it; I drank wine but only one glass per day (making sure I stayed in control); I took my meds, which helped numb everything, including the physical pain; and I watched a lot of TV. If I wasn't working, I watched TV; that was all I did. I stopped living and was only existing. Eventually I lost my job and my house, and I didn't care.

I found another job I could hide in. This job allowed me to just go to work and go home; I didn't have any responsibility once I left work. I focused on the people from work, I focused on my daughter and my grandkids, but I kept my distance as far as getting too close. In early 2011 I knew things had to change and I couldn't continue to hide from life. My son was not coming back, and my life just kept getting harder and harder. So I began walking again. I would walk several times a day. I walked around the block, and then I would do it again. My dog George (who passed away a short time later) would look at me like I was crazy, but as I would grab his leash for the third or fourth time, he would get up to go without hesitation. Maybe I was crazy, but things started to change. I started feeling emotions again, I started wanting things I hadn't cared about for a long time, I started to taste food, and I started to want more out of life. I also began thinking about my own life and how disappointed my son would be with me. I was not the same person who had raised him, and I knew that if I wanted to honor his memory and his life, I needed to get back to living.

Whenever I would walk, I would gain more insight and attachment to life. I started thinking and making decisions. I stopped doing status quo and avoiding life. I started to feel again, and some of the feelings were very difficult to feel. I had buried anger and guilt; I had put being sad on a shelf and stuck it way back out of the way. The pain I felt I had learned to numb out, and it was all coming back. I was walking and thinking and planning and beginning to find some peace in all of it. I didn't know why everything that had happened did happen, but I believed that life is a lot bigger than any of us imagine and for whatever reason there was something in all of the loss that needed to happen. I believed there is a grander scheme. Not knowing the end result has never been my strength, but I had to have faith that there was an end result to all of this.

I started talking to peers; I went to a counselor and began getting and asking for help once again. It is healing to talk about things and have someone to validate what you are feeling. It is healing to talk to someone who has a view from the outside. I began to heal and move forward, and life started feeling better.

Life is a work in progress, and we all have stories that have shaped who we are and how we live. The events that shape you can either control your life or help you continue to grow and learn. The events will never stop happening, but your reaction to these events is a choice every one of us has. Staying numb and never allowing anyone to ever get close to me again was one way to deal with my son's death; however, it also would have kept me in victim thinking.

Victim thinking is the type of thinking that says, "If this would not have happened to me, then life would be like this." It gives an excuse for why things are so bad. If I would have stayed in victim thinking, I would have used my son's death as an excuse, and that would be so disappointing to the person he was as well as a disappointment to myself. I don't like what happened; I miss him every day, and I would give anything to see him and hear him again. I keep his memory close and talk about who he was often. He brought so much happiness to my life, and I feel blessed to have had him in my life. That will never change.

Asking for help from friends, family, and professionals is very helpful. It does not mean I am weak; it means that I am gaining strength. I know asking for help can feel awkward and vulnerable, but you will be better for doing it. You can get out of being stuck and begin to move forward. Asking for help also gives others permission to ask for help. It has a ripple effect, and you never know who you may end up affecting by you taking the first step.

This is part of moving. Moving does not only mean your physical body; it also means mentally and emotionally. Your body can only move where the mind is focused. If you are focused on negativity, resentments, regrets, grudges, or loss, then your body will respond in this way. This response usually looks like drinking, avoiding, isolating, overworking, or overindulging in things that are not healthy. This will make it very difficult to get moving. If you focus on the present moment, getting up and walking or moving somehow does not seem so overwhelming. If you can give yourself ten minutes every day, you will see improvement in your life. If you can give yourself this ten minutes every day, over time you will see improvement in moods, thoughts, emotional regulation, and the ability to deal with problems in life. Don't allow the past to take over your present moment. Life is full of challenges, and it is full of joy. Give yourself the gift of movement. If you have physical problems that keep you from moving, then get outside and enjoy the sounds and sights; go to a park or look around and see what is going on around you. Let yourself appreciate life. Focus on the moment; that is all you have. Get up and move to improve your moods, improve your thoughts, and get living.

Chapter 11

Mental Health Tip #11: A meditation
practice has been known to change
lives. This healing method *works*!

Whenever I introduce meditation to clients, I get the same initial reaction. First, there is the rolling of the eyes or the look that says I am crazy. Then come all the reasons why it would never work for them. And then there is the statement, "Well maybe I could try it." Most of the time you don't like to do things you are not good at or try things that other people may think are weird. Most of us do not like change either. So, many times the excuses go like this: "I have tried it, and my thoughts go crazy," "I don't like that hippie-dippie crap; it is hogwash," "I don't have time," "I read about it and tried meditation, but it made things worse," or "I don't believe in God or religion." Now these are just a few of the excuses I have heard. There are many more; however, they all fall under those general statements somewhere. Here is what I tell them because it is important to have full information about meditation and what it can do to improve life.

Meditation is not about religion, and it's not about making your thoughts disappear. Meditation could be considered hippy, I suppose, but if you were able to calm down your reactions to stress, have more control over eating patterns, make better decisions in those high emotional times, and just have an overall awareness of life, would it be worth learning to meditate? If you are concerned with what others think about you, then there are some things that may need to be addressed so that you can live your life being yourself without fearing what others will think if you try new things. Meditation can actually help you become less fearful and anxious. Being in charge of your life means you make decisions based on what you need and what you want out of life. Being in charge of your life means that your thoughts and emotions are not controlling your behavior. Being in charge of your life means that what others think about what you are doing for your life is really none of your business; how the changes you make in your life will affect other people, however, will be positive. If you are living true to the values you believe in, then your decisions will have a positive effect on others.

As I write these words, I remember what I thought about meditation before I began the daily practice. I had tried it several times but could not get my brain to stop chatting. I have a constant committee that is in a continual meeting in my brain, and my thoughts go crazy so much of the time. I could not focus for more than a few seconds. I got frustrated and eventually said, "This isn't for me." Of course, that kicked in my rebelliousness. I wasn't going to let this get the best of me. I had read all of the benefits, I had known people who seemed so at peace with life, and their answer was a daily meditation practice. Nobody had told me I needed to do this, which I think was good, because then I would have had to prove them wrong and show them I didn't need meditation in my life. The only person I was fighting with was myself, as usual.

I began researching ways to meditate. I found out that there is not just one way to meditate; there are many, so finding one that I connected with made sense to me and helped me get past my preconceived notion about what meditation was. This began my journey of learning to meditate, which I want to pass on to you.

What I have found is that the biggest part of meditation is starting. So I began—again. I started trying different types of meditations. I started with guided imagery meditation, which was good because I could visualize the beach and the sun and sand because it is one of my favorite places. Guided imagery meditation is generally listening to someone take you to a place in your mind that is peaceful. You can find CDs of this type of meditation, and you can also find this type of meditation online. There are many websites that offer guided imagery meditations. Once I found this meditation and felt like I could do it, I started looking for other types of meditations. I couldn't believe how many there are.

I found progressive muscle meditation, which I actually really liked. I also found that I could do this type of meditation because my brain was busy focusing on the muscle group. This type of meditation is one that you begin with breathing, and as you take a deep breath in, you tighten muscles in one area of your body; when you exhale you relax the muscle group. You may start with the top part of your body like your arms and then work down until you have done every major muscle group. The last part of this meditation is tightening your whole body as you breathe in, and then when you exhale, you relax your whole body and then just let your body breathe for a bit. This type of meditation is especially good if you have a hard time falling asleep because you can do it in your bed, and by the time you are at the end of all muscle groups and letting your body breathe, you may find yourself sleeping. It is also very helpful if you are having a stressful day and need to de-stress, or if you deal with chronic pain. I tried this meditation to see about getting some relief from RA symptoms, and it really helped.

Another meditation I found was a breathing meditation. This one takes more focus, but as you build your daily meditation practice, it is amazing to see how much more control you have over focusing or, rather, defocusing. To do this type of meditation, you begin by taking a deep breath in, counting to four; you then hold this breath for the count of four, and then slowly let your breath out for a count of four; you then hold that for a count of four, and then begin another cycle by taking another deep breath for the count of four. You can start by doing this for four or five cycles, and you have just meditated for a minute. This is a very good way to learn to meditate and focus on your breathing because once you are able to focus on your breath, when you are in a stressful situation, you can focus on your breath and immediately de-stress or calm down. This is a good meditation to practice because you will end up using this skill in many instances, as I do.

As you begin to build a meditation practice, you may want to try some of the more traditional styles of meditation. These meditations use the lotus sitting position (sitting cross-legged) and putting your right hand on top of your left in a cup position, with palms facing up. Essentially your left hand is cupping your right hand. Then you bring your thumbs together, which makes a triangle. Your hands rest in your lap. As you are sitting there, you want to feel balanced and unobstructed as you sit, so find a position where you don't feel strain in your neck or back, your shoulders are relaxed, and your head is sitting balanced without feeling any strain. Close your eyes and begin taking deep breaths. As you breathe in, you think of one word or phrase. Many people who do this meditation use "om" as the phrase, but you can use any word or phrase that you connect with. Once you are in a good position, you begin by closing your eyes and breathing slowly. Once you have taken a couple of deep cleansing breaths, begin to say the word or phrase over and over again. You can do this along with your breathing or just focus on the word and allow your body to breathe naturally.

One thing to remember about meditation—whether you are focusing on breathing or doing progressive muscle meditation or guided imagery—your brain may start thinking and drifting off, which can feel frustrating. This is normal. When you find yourself focused on a work problem or a conversation you had with a friend or colleague, you only need to notice the thought, acknowledge it in a sense, and continue with the meditation. I have found myself in a meditation and focusing on work. I notice the thought and then refocus on breathing or the phrase I am saying. Once again it is about practice, learning to notice your emotions and your thoughts without trying to fix them or react to them.

There are many different types of meditation, and finding one that you can do takes a little research and trial and error. There is not a right and a wrong way to meditate; it is only about practice and progress. Meditation has become part of my daily morning routine, and I know it has made a difference in my life and how I handle my emotions, stressful events, drama from other people, emotional eating to try to feel better, fitness or lack thereof, and general life balance. Meditation is a way to connect to something internal instead of all of the external things that you may be using to feel connected. These external things, like food, alcohol, TV, movies, gaming, sex, or work, will not bring the same satisfaction that learning to effectively take charge of your life brings.

Being open to try new things is part of the experience of life; give yourself a challenge to try meditation daily for thirty days. Are you already saying no? Ask yourself what excuses you have thought of already to not try meditation. What are you saying to yourself about meditation right now that will keep you from trying it? Is your mind open, or have you already shut the idea down? Try meditation for thirty days—what have you got to lose? If you do not see benefits after thirty days, then go back to the way you handled life before you began the meditation challenge. The only thing you would have lost in this thirty-day challenge is nothing.

Trying a meditation practice could change your life. Remember that if you want life to change, it takes changing one thing. Meditation could be the one thing that could help you improve your life and create the changes you are looking for. It is your attitude that will hold you back from changing. Remember, you can teach an old dog a new trick. If you truly want change in your life, you will be open to changing something. You can try the thirty-day challenge and see what happens. If you never try it, you will never know how meditation can benefit your life.

Chapter 12

Mental Health Tip #12: Doing the opposite of what you think or feel may help you get into the solution.

Doing the opposite of what you think or feel may sound like a crazy concept, but as I explain what I mean by doing the opposite, hopefully it will make more sense. Think of the last time you were driving down a very busy street and it was bumper-to-bumper traffic. Now picture yourself being in a hurry to get somewhere and being stuck in that traffic. What do see yourself doing? Are you yelling at the car in front of you, or are you squeezing the steering wheel tight and rocking back and forth? Are you smacking the steering wheel? Are you calling a friend and complaining about the traffic? Are you thinking about food or thinking about the good stiff drink you will be having soon to calm down? Picture what it looks like for you in this type of stressful moment.

Picturing how you respond to an event like a traffic jam is a good way to see the way you handle stress in your life. What this means is that if you picture yourself being loud, turning the music up, and hitting the steering wheel or if you picture yourself getting food or an alcoholic beverage to calm down, then this is probably what you do when any stressful event comes into your life. This might sound crazy, but here is why it is a good exercise to do.

We tend to handle situations in our life with the same type of coping skills we have used for most of our life. If I use alcohol to deal with the crazy day I just had, I will probably be thinking about alcohol when I am sitting in a traffic jam too. If I tend to use my loud voice to handle situations in my life, I will probably be yelling in my car at other people in their cars. We tend to deal with stuff that happens in the same patterns and habits that have helped us in the past. If food is my go-to, then I may be thinking about the drive-through I will be going to as soon as I get out of this traffic.

Ken was recently divorced and used alcohol to deal with the stress and anxiety he felt from the divorce. He would deal with anxiety by taking the prescriptions that the doctor prescribed to him; however, he would use more than prescribed. He was successful at his job, and he had high expectations for people he worked with to be successful too. He held everyone to a high standard. He had been married for many years and had two children, who, he adored. He would come home to his wife and kids and retreat to his man cave (so to speak), where he would drink his evening away. He would say good night to his kids, and then he would get on the computer or watch sports or news until he could go to bed. In the morning he would get up and do it all again. When his wife informed him that she wanted a divorce, he was shocked, but when he found out she had been seeing someone else, he was devastated. He had thought that his lifestyle was perfect but found out that this was a lie.

When you begin to reevaluate your life, you may sometimes find out things are not as they might appear. So many times the life that looks perfect is anything but perfect. When the focus is on what a person looks like on the outside, what the children look like, dress like, and behave like, it can be devastation when reality hits. It would be great to think that life was perfect and that having a perfect wife, children, cars, homes, and vacations meant that life really was perfect. But having the big house, nice cars, and all of the big toys does not make life perfect.

For many, having this perfect-looking life is a way to avoid. When you start digging into what is really happening, you start finding out that the relationships are strained or nonexistent, there is hurt or pain from the past, and material things have become one way to feel better. From the outside everything seems good, but on the inside, life feels dark, heavy, or just blah. Most of us will try to portray an image of how we want others to see us. This image becomes a way of life, and eventually knowing who you really are is covered up by this image. A perfect life or whatever image is being portrayed becomes the focus, which takes away from actually living and learning to enjoy life and those small moments.

Ken had a perfect-looking life. He had a nice home, nice cars, and a wife who could stay home and take care of all the daily things that were important to him. He always knew that when he came home, everything would be perfect. He began to realize why looking perfect was so important to him. He was more interested in what others thought about his lifestyle and looking perfect than he was about feeling his life. He began considering why he wanted his life to look this way. He became more honest about his marriage, and figured out that his marriage was more about the image than it was about the relationship with his wife. He started thinking that he married her because she fit the mold of what he thought a perfect wife was. He loved her but was unsure whether he loved her for who she was or loved her because she fit his plan. He began questioning what he thought love was. This realization began to unravel years of having to be perfect, and when things did not look perfect, he would self-destruct by drinking more.

Ken put a lot of pressure on himself. If he played sports, he had to be the best so he could play at the level he expected of himself. He always had to show his dad that he was better than his older brothers, even though he never really believed he was better. He believed his dad always spent more time with his brothers, so he would constantly up the expectations for himself to get his dad to notice him. He had never talked to his dad about this but just assumed this was what Dad always thought. He decided he needed to talk to his dad. He wanted to see if what he thought of his relationship was actually true or if it was just more of the pressure he put on himself. He asked his dad to go have lunch so they could sit down and talk. For the first time in his life, he actually talked to his dad. He found out that his dad never had high expectations; he just tried to stay out of his son's way because Ken would get so frustrated when things didn't go well. So his dad learned to let him figure it out, be a cheerleader from the background, and stay out of his way. Ken learned that his dad was always amazed at and proud of him. Dad had become a silent cheerleader. Ken thought he had to be perfect to get the approval of his dad, and since he never really felt like he had Dad's approval, he kept pushing himself and others to make a perfect-looking life.

Ken reevaluated his life and started seeing things differently after this. He started talking to his kids differently and not worrying about how they did things. He began to play with them instead of watch them play. He started dating again but was looking for a partner and friend instead of someone who could fit a mold. His life started changing. He was no longer mad about his ex-wife because he took responsibility for his part in their failed marriage. He began to see that if he would have treated his wife like a friend and a partner instead of an image, maybe they would still be married. He found that if he would have been really honest with her when they were dating, then it was possible they would not have gotten married. It is difficult to be this honest about our lives, but learning to be this honest with your own life is what allows the healing to take place, forgiveness to happen, and life to change.

There are events in our life that rock our world, and we have a tendency to hold on with as much control as possible so that other people won't see our hurt and vulnerability. This type of control will generally bury what is honest and allows you to justify the actions or behaviors you are using to feel better. I also had one of those moments that rocked my world and made me change the way I lived. I remember breaking down into tears and realizing that I had been living a lie for a very long time. The reason I kept living this lie was because so much of what I was doing was a part of the lie or the image. I was trying to be a certain person who had a certain lifestyle; however, it was not really who I was or am today. Once that moment comes when you begin to evaluate your life and start seeing things you are doing that are not part of who you are, change will happen.

The answer lies in being honest about your actions, being responsible and accountable for what you have done in your life, and then doing something about it. So many times you want to look at the other people in your life and blame them for your life or lack thereof, but the only person to blame is yourself. Our life is our responsibility and nobody else's. Everything that happens in your life, you had a part to play. Being honest about your part is freeing because it allows you to repair, resolve, and fix the parts of your life that are broken. If you are blaming someone else for your life, then you have given this person control of your life.

When I realized that I was using shopping and spending money as a way to make things better and spending more money than I had, I had no one to blame but myself. It was time to start being honest and fix what I had done. It took a very long time to undo the financial damage I had done, but it felt so much better than what

I had been doing that it became motivating. I couldn't blame the credit card companies, the bank, or whom I owed money to. This allowed me to be responsible and fix my finances. I had to be honest about my actions and honest about my solutions. I didn't have to spend money to feel better; being honest, coming up with a plan, and then taking action from this plan allowed me to feel better.

If the way you respond to life is by stuffing away everything you think and feel and then eating, drinking, smoking, spending money, viewing pornography, or working, then maybe it is time to try something different. Going to talk to someone where you can be open and honest or writing down everything that has happened during the day, week, or month that has brought you stress are ways that help you get your feelings out. It is not healthy to keep all of the stress and pressure from life inside. When you keep it inside, you usually use unhealthy coping skills to feel better. These unhealthy coping skills will only feel better in the moment, but the guilt of overeating or drinking too much or having one-night stands or affairs will ultimately make you feel worse. When you feel like this, then you want to hide it from others, so you work on the stories and the deceptions to keep others from finding out how you are coping with life. These deceptions grow like weeds, and so the need to continue to binge-eat, drink more, or have more sex becomes even greater until you are lost in the world of lies and deceit. This cycle will become the normal way of life, and most of the time you don't even see the destructive pattern because you are too busy living it.

When you begin to take a step back and reevaluate your life, you can then start doing the opposite of what you normally would do and do something different. So when I would avoid problems or stress in my life, I spent money and tried to keep up certain financial appearances. I was so unaware of the mess I was making that when it finally caught up to me, I was devastated. This was when I started evaluating my life and what I was doing, which resulted in an overwhelming feeling of disappointment and disgust. That was the day my life changed. I stopped blaming the bills on someone else, I stopped blaming the credit card bill on the credit card company (after all, I was the one who used the card), I stopped avoiding paying medical bills and other bills that I kept putting off, and I started paying down my debt. I quit spending money, I sold my car and bought a very cheap car that my kids called the cream puff. I sold other material things that I thought made me feel better but really didn't, and I got out of the financial mess I was in. I started feeling better on the inside, instead of making myself look better from the outside. When you want to change your life, you have to change the way you normally do things. So doing the opposite of what you normally do can help you improve your life and begin a positive change and life improvement.

Chapter 13

Mental Health Tip #13: Simple moments bring
the best memories; enjoy those simple times.

Life is full of memories; some memories bring a lot of joy, and other
memories bring a lot of hurt. One thing I have learned recently is
that simple moments bring the biggest smiles. As I look back on
my life and remember all of the vacations, the work, the family
events, the family drama, fun times with friends, and times that
have changed the direction of my life, the one thing that seems to
hold it all together is the simple moments. I remember sitting on
my grandparents' deck eating popsicles that my grandma would
make from juice, and just being happy to be there. Grandpa would
sing songs that he taught us as kids. These songs will pop up at
times in my life and in my thoughts and bring me comfort. After
my grandpa passed away, these songs would come into my thoughts
at odd times of stress, and these small moments helped me get
through some really stressful times. The songs, the moments on my
grandparents' deck, the popsicles are all small moments that created
lasting memories. Times like these are not really thought about
until they are gone. We don't learn to sit back and breathe in these
moments and enjoy. It is time to enjoy these moments and realize

that these are the moments that make up life. It is not the new car, house, boat, or TV; it is the moments that happen while boating or eating popcorn watching a movie on the new TV.

It is amazing how many of these moments there are. When I think about many of these moments, I probably was worrying about a bill, an argument, what to cook for dinner, how to get the better car, how to keep up with friends who seemed to have it all, or so many other worries that really did not matter anyway. The bill I was worried about ended up being paid, the dinner got cooked, the argument was resolved, and the friends did not really care. Worrying about other stuff instead of being in the moment let all of these things rent space in my head and take away from experiencing those moments. Looking back, I wasted a lot of energy by not living in the moment.

Living in the moment takes practice. Our society has taught us that to get pleasure and happiness, we must have and do everything. If you have the house, the car, a boat or a four-wheeler, credit cards, the newest phone, a gaming system, the big television, and a nice body, and can go out, then things must be going well. This is the lie we are fed. The fact is that happiness comes from within. When someone is actually happy, he or she can be happy anywhere, anytime, and in any situation. It is not the perfect mate, the best stuff, or the newest technology that will make you happy. All of the outside stuff will bring pressure, stress, and an image to live up to. This image brings with it a need to control. This perceived control is so many times what will lead you to do things you would never normally do.

I have always had the gift of listening. Even as a young child, I was the one who listened, I wasn't the outgoing child; I was the quiet introvert. I am blessed to be a sounding board and would not have it any other way. I believe that sharing our lives is healing as well as necessary. People tend to keep secrets for a very long time, and what I have learned is that secrets will keep you sick. This type of sickness is physical, mental, emotional, and spiritual.

Beverly was a woman who kept secrets. She had a good job and a nice home, with nice furnishings, a nice car, nice clothes, and jewelry, but she was not happy. She could not understand why she was so miserable. She was very successful and had to do things she did not necessarily like to get where she was in her career. She had to say and do things that she didn't really feel good about, but it got her promotions. She was one of the main directors in her company and hated her life. She started realizing she was keeping up an image that she hated. She had everything she could possibly want but realized this was just stuff to help her avoid herself. She shopped, drank wine, had many one-night stands, and worked to avoid being alone with herself. She hated spending time alone and would avoid it at all costs. She would spend money on things she did not want or need to keep up the appearances. She was unable to sleep, so she would drink wine until she would pass out. She had gotten several DUIs from drinking and driving, but it didn't stop her from doing it over and over. She eventually lost her job and her relationship with her children because of this lifestyle. She drank and drove so many times she quit thinking about it. She was able to get out of her first DUI. The next one she did some classes online to satisfy the court, but her last DUI was when she lost her job. The people she worked with wouldn't help her anymore. Her children would not talk to her, and the men she slept with began disappearing. When the shit hit the fan, it hit with a vengeance.

Beverly went to see professionals to help her and was on the road to recovery. She was a broken woman who would put on a smile and act like everything was all right even though she was in pain from everything that had happened in her life. She quit drinking, was spending time with the one man whom she really cared about, and began working on her relationship with her kids. Her life was not as flashy, but she began enjoying her life. She began doing the hard work, and her life began to change.

When you begin to look into a mirror and realize that what happened to you is your own doing, it can be a devastating realization. However, this can be the first step to healing your life. When people face what they have done to themselves, it opens the door to begin to change the direction of their life. In order for life to change, something in life has to change. This can only begin from within. Nobody can make us change or make us decide to change. This is a decision that each of us gets to make. The only way to change is to be honest and open and begin to unravel the mess that has been created. In order to rebuild, you have to sometimes start over, and this is very challenging. So many of our journeys are the same, but each of us reacts to our situations differently. The ability to be open and honest is the first step to changing a life.

There are many stories of people who have survived. Other people's stories can be information on how you can take that first step toward change. Most of us do not know where to begin or how to stop the facade of the life that has been created. This first step is challenging, and it can be overwhelming. We all have a story to share, and when you share your story, it allows others to know that it is okay to share their story. You may feel vulnerable, but vulnerability takes strength and strength changes lives. The ability to survive very difficult situations is amazing; it just does not feel amazing.

There are so many people who have lost relationships with their children, parents, siblings, spouses, adult children, and friends. So many people don't even realize that it is happening until the damage is done. Losing jobs, losing family, and losing relationships can be devastating, especially when it is our own doing. It is easier to use alcohol, food, sex, gambling, prescription pills, or drugs to numb the pain than it is to take responsibility and try to fix the mistakes that were made. As long as there is alcohol, there is no need to think about all the destruction. Most of us lose so much in what may seem like a short amount of time, but the reality is the destruction had been happening for a long time; it just took time for the destructive path to come to a head and blow up.

When you begin to evaluate all of the layers that you may be covering up by buying things, drinking, or having many sexual partners without actually connecting to any of them, you may realize that using men or women to feel wanted and desirable will only work for so long. Some of these people may help you climb the ladder of success, and some may actually be hurting your ability to be successful. The problem is that sometimes it is hard to know the difference. If you are using people for distractions or that instant gratification, it will ultimately end up hurting you. Being lonely and drinking wine and having sex will keep you from feeling lonely for a while. The wine can help you escape from thinking, feeling, and living, but eventually it will not be enough.

When this is how you live, it is not possible to live and enjoy the small moments. Life becomes consumed with keeping up with the image that has been created. Trying to stay ahead of this image is exhausting. However, when you are living like this, you do not know how exhausting it is until something happens that intervenes. In the previous story, Beverly had three DUIs, which became the intervention to stop her in her tracks and begin the reevaluation of her life. The first two she was able to avoid and keep on going, even though these were warning signs. When this happens, it is an opportunity to change things or an opportunity to make things worse. She took the road to make things worse, and it got much worse. The last DUI she could not get out of; it was no longer a slap on the wrist, but was a wake-up call. She had to do something different because the choices were limited.

It may take a while after the intervention comes to start taking responsibility for your actions and looking at the way you are living. There is generally a lot of shame and guilt for the way you may be living. This guilt and shame can either drive you further down the road of destruction, or you can learn to forgive and begin to pick up the pieces. Learn to be open to the process of healing. Everything that may feel broken can be fixed; however, it may take a lot of work to get others to trust you again. This process can be a long one, but with each step, your life can improve.

Learning to live in the simple moments and enjoy what you are doing in those moments can take a lot of practice. Letting go of all the worries and stresses of life and being present in the moment allows you to enjoy what is happening now. The image that so many people live is a farce—trying to keep up with an illusion of bigger, better, and more, more, more. This will not create happiness; this will only create stress and the inability to enjoy what you do have. If you started listing the things in your life that you are grateful for, you might find that everything that makes you happy is something external, such as alcohol, sex, cars, and the like. If your list looks like this, it may be time for a change. Learning to enjoy simple moments lets you be present in life, and when you are present in life and in the moment, there are really no problems or issues. Sounds crazy, right?

In the present moment, there are no problems. There are problems in the future to worry about and there are problems from the past to worry about, but right now in the present moment, there are no problems; there is only now. We tend to make problems worse by the way we future trip or continue to think and catastrophize what has happened in the past. Right now there is only right now and nothing more. Enjoying right now makes all of those problems not a problem. Right now is not thinking about future issues, and it is not thinking about past problems; it is just now, this minute, this second. In this very moment you can choose to work on what you are doing right now, or you can focus on what may or may not happen in the future. There is no control over the future; there is only control with what you choose to do right now.

Try to remember that simple moments are what you will remember when you look back on life. Simple moments are what you remember when someone in your life dies, and simple moments are what you will remember as you look back on your children's life or your own childhood. Will you be able to look back and remember those simple times, or will you look back and remember the problems from that year or time in your life? I encourage you to take time every day and find something to appreciate, take time to feel what is going on without having to drown it in alcohol or sex, take time to see the beauty of living the experiences of life, which are full of moments to feel and to share. Life is full of ups and downs, and each one gives you an experience. Learn to be okay with feeling the experience of life as it happens because you only get that moment to experience it; after that it is in the past.

Chapter 14

A Look into Grief

I wanted to add a section about grief because prior to 2005, I knew only what I had learned in graduate school and workshops on grief and loss. I didn't know anything about what really happens with grief. I lost my grandparents within three months of each other. This happened in December 2005 when my grandpa passed away quite suddenly, and by February 2006 my grandma passed away. These were the grandparents who made homemade popsicles that we would eat while sitting on their deck. These were the grandparents who I had seen weekly for the better part of my life. I missed them dearly. Losing both of them in a matter of months was quite difficult because things changed. I didn't like the change to holidays or family get-togethers; it was all so different.

My grandparents' dying was the first real experience I had with the death of someone I was very close with. Then on August 11, 2008, my son died in a fatal car accident. He died in the hospital while they were trying to save his life. I went through a divorce within a month of losing my son, and then I lost my job in December 2010. My dog George died in December 2011, my stepfather died

January 2012, and my brother's father-in-law died one month later. My stepbrother died within a year of stepdad. One of my best friends died September 2012, and instead of going on a camping trip to Colorado with him, I went to his funeral.

My mom and stepdad had been married since I was ten, and my stepbrother was one of five stepbrothers and stepsisters. He was the one I knew the most and had been the closest to. My family had gotten together for Sunday dinners for a very long time. These dinners included my brother's in-laws. So when my brother's father-in-law passed away from cancer, it was one more devastation to the family. I was fairly numb by the time my stepdad and my brother father-in–law died, and the funerals are really a blur. I was going through the motions and trying to protect myself from feeling any more losses.

Grief came in waves, I became numb, and I barely remember Dad's funeral. I had not actually been able to come to terms with losing my son, and in the years that followed his death, I really don't remember having any emotion or feeling. I don't remember enjoying any part of life; however I don't remember not enjoying life either. I was on autopilot. I remember getting up, going to a job where I didn't have to think too much or give much of myself, going home, helping take care of my grandkids who were toddlers at the time, talking to my daughter, and then going to bed. After Ryan (my son) passed away my daughter and grandchildren moved in with me. We lived together to help each other get through this time. This was my life in which I was existing. I was not able to deal with any pressures. I would be asked by friends to go places, and I would decline. I mostly wanted to be at home; this felt safe. I did what I had to do to survive and pay bills, but that was it. If I was home I was in my pajamas with no plans other than watching TV, playing with my grandkids in the backyard or inside, and waiting to go to sleep. Sleep was my relief. I sometimes would have dreams with my kiddo in them and would wake up in tears because I wanted so badly for these to be real. I would want to sleep because maybe, just maybe, I would dream and he would be there. But I would wake up and remember that he wasn't.

I learned about the stages of grief in graduate school, and the stages made so much sense that when I would counsel people who were grieving over a loss of a husband, father, or job, I would talk about the stages and have clients talk about the stage of grief they were experiencing. When I experienced grief, I realized that there is more to grief than stages. There are varying levels of grief. The grief I felt when Stepdad died was different from the grief I felt when my son Ryan died. The grief I felt for my grandparents was different from either my stepdad or my son, and the grief for my dog was again different from any of the other losses.

I remember wishing at times that I wouldn't wake up. I remember being disappointed in the morning when I woke up that I did wake up. It was a time of being disengaged from life. It was a time of not getting close to anyone because I could not bear to think I would lose someone else. I could not feel or take anymore. Most of the people who knew me did not know how I was doing because I would put on a smile. I would talk about how much I missed those who had left, but really the only one who knew how hard it was for me was my daughter, who was dealing with the loss of her brother the best way she could. We would talk about him, the accident, memories we each had, and how different it would be if he were still here.

I would do things with my grandkids and try to be okay so they would not know the difference. I remember going to the dog park after George died with my other dog and talking to someone who told me I looked sad. He asked me if I was okay, and I told him it was just a rough couple of years. We shared stories about the loss of people in our lives and how different life was today because of it. He said, "Your daughter and grandkids, especially your son's kids, need you here." I had told myself this, but when he said it, I actually heard it. It took a while for this to sink in, but eventually I did start doing a few things.

I tried going for a hike with a meetup group I had found. My younger brother went with me, and it was nice to get out. I still did not feel anything like I used to feel. It was nice to get out, but that was it. I went out at night a few times, but again it was just okay; I did not feel that excitement of getting ready and looking forward to seeing a concert or meeting new people—everything just felt the exact same okay. It is hard to describe what life felt like, but the only word that seems to describe it is gray. I knew I had work to do to pick myself up, but I just wasn't sure I wanted to. This is where the honesty comes in and the decision gets made.

Grief still comes in waves. There are days that are really difficult, and there are days that are good. I have had to fight hard to get back among the living. Just doing one thing at a time and learning to live again in a world that is very different than I ever thought it would be. I would never have imagined my life like this ten or fifteen years ago.

Grief does have stages of anger, depression, bargaining, denial, and acceptance (Kübler-Ross model); however, I also believe there are varying degrees or levels of grief. I have found myself in each of these stages and still have moments of anger and depression. I have more acceptance over the loss of my son and all the losses that followed his death. I have had to journal, walk and exercise, meditate, talk to a professional, talk to family, and push myself to heal. I had to learn to live the healing process and allow things to unfold. This has not been a quick journey or one that I could just ignore. I remember asking myself one day, "Am I willing to walk the walk, or do I just talk the talk?" I had to be honest and tell myself right now I was talking the talk and it was time to walk the walk. This was a very hard day.

When I began, my fear was that maybe I would forget. What was I thinking I would forget? Was I afraid I would forget my son? Was I afraid I would forget the memories? Was I afraid I would forget the pain? Yes, that was it; I was afraid that if I forgot the pain that I would once again let myself get close to someone and I could potentially feel that overwhelming loss again. I was also afraid that if I forgot the pain that his death would not mean anything and maybe other people would not understand how I could enjoy life after I lost my son. After all, a parent is not supposed to outlive his or her children. As I began to evaluate my thought process and what I was hanging on to, I realized that all I wanted was to remember the good times with my son, be grateful for the twenty-six years he had on this earth and being a part of his journey, and enjoy his family, my daughter and her family, and the rest of my family. I wanted to make sure that his memory was not about his death but about his life. I wanted to honor his memory by living and not existing. It has been a long journey, and I am here to tell you that grief is a journey and everyone deals with grief in his or her own way. There is no right or wrong to grief. It is your process.

If you have experienced the loss of someone you are close to and you are finding yourself just existing, do not give up on life. Allow yourself to just be okay with your process. Talk to friends and professionals about the loss. Find simple things that will allow you to relearn how to live after the loss. Do not think that there is a time frame about how fast or how slow your process is. Do not let others tell you what you should or should not be doing. Many people may not understand why you are not over it yet. Do not take this personally; many times people may not understand what you are going through. Do not judge yourself about your process. Do take time to remember. Do take time to go to special places where you spent time with your loved one. Do journal and write about what you are going through. Writing is a way to get out thoughts and feelings that sometimes are not making a lot of sense to others. Do draw or use artwork as a way to deal with your grief. Do something for yourself weekly that will help you. Allow the process and give yourself permission to feel whatever you are feeling in that moment.

I understand grief more than I really ever wanted to. I have gained compassion, love, and a deeper awareness of life. I have become more spiritual and have a true belief about life after death. Death is a part of life. Life is a journey of experiences. Each of these experiences helps to make up the person you are. Your experiences are unique to you because you are the only one who is experiencing what you are experiencing. Other people have gone through similar experiences, but their experiences are theirs. It is impossible to understand exactly how someone feels since that is unique to him or her. Our emotions and thoughts and even circumstances may be similar, and this gives us the ability to empathize with fellow humans; however, the process in which you deal with your experience is unique to you and no one else. Do not judge others for their process. Empathize because you understand what it is like to lose someone. Empathize because you know what it is like to lose a job, go through a divorce, break up with a boyfriend or girlfriend, move away from your best friend, lose a promotion to a colleague, or lose the house you have lived in. Grief can be felt from many different experiences.

It is important to recognize the stages of grief so you are not just responding and reacting to these stages. It is also important to understand the triggers that can throw your day or week off. You may go by a place not thinking anything about it and begin feeling aggravated or just off somehow without understanding where these feelings are coming from. If you backtrack the last twenty-four hours or so, you may find you went by a place that you often went with your loved one. This triggered emotions without you even realizing what was happening. As you begin to understand some of the places, people, or even certain days of a certain month that have a triggering effect on your emotions, you can better take care of yourself, and you won't feel the need to do something that is self-destructive by doing or saying something that may be hurtful to you or someone else. You will be able to remind yourself that you miss your loved one.

Learn about your process, understand your triggers, and don't be too hard on yourself. Don't compare yourself to other people and how they are doing. It is rare that what someone is showing on the outside is what is happening on the inside. Learn to talk and be open about what you are going through to those you trust. This life is really something, and if you find yourself living for days of the past, maybe it is time to look at the day you are currently in. Notice the sunset and sunrise, notice the moon or stars, notice the clouds or the laughs of your children or grandchildren—just start noticing something that is happening in this day and in this moment to remind yourself that there is more. Recognizing some of the gifts that you have in this moment can help you experience living again. After loss it is difficult to want to live in a world that is so different; it is easier to exist and think about the good times from the past.

Remember to take care of yourself by being gentle. Be gentle with your grief process, be gentle with your emotions and thoughts, and be gentle with others who do not understand. Remember that after loss your world will look and feel different. Finding a way to live in this different world takes time.

Chapter 15

Thoughts about Mental Health

Mental health is a part of life; however, mental health is rarely considered in anyone's life. When mental health is considered, it is generally under some type of duress or crisis. I saw a comic strip the other day that portrayed our society's consideration toward mental health. It went a little like this to show how things would be if physical health was treated the way mental health is: A man lying in bed is shivering with the flu. His partner is telling him that if he would get up, he would probably feel better. Another window showed a doctor listening to a patient's heart and saying, "If you just ignore the sound, it will go away." There was another window where a man taking medications was being told by his friend that taking medications every day isn't healthy, and he should be worried that it was changing who he was.

This was just a comic strip, but it was a very real depiction of the stigma that the mental health field has. The problem is that this stigma keeps a lot of people from seeking help for feeling depressed, anxious, or unable to cope with life stressors without being self-destructive. There is not a person on the planet who does not deal with mental health issues during his or her life. Some people may have better coping skills, but everyone deals with mental health.

Mental health is not separate from who you are, it is not separate from your physical or emotional health, and it is not separate from your social or relationship health, your spiritual health, or your financial health. Mental health is part of the whole, and if it is ignored, it will affect all other areas of your life. Taking care of yourself means that you are taking care of your mental health as well as the other areas of life. The mental health tips in this book are to help you find some coping skills that will improve your mental health.

You may not connect with all of the mental health tips in this book, but if you find one or two that will assist you in improving your mental health, that means life would improve. Moving forward in life means that you are looking for ways to improve your overall health and well-being, which then transfers to the outside world and improves your overall daily living.

Remembering that emotions come and go and getting through the intense emotional state without reacting to what got you there in the first place can help you improve relationships. Remember that life is constantly changing and you can't control everything in your life. Learning to let go or let it be can help you relieve anxiety. Remembering that living in the day and not focusing on the past or the future can help you get done what you need to every day to reach your goals and decrease depressed and anxious moods. Learning to meditate and be still every day will not only retrain your brain to respond more proactively; it will help you find peace and comfort in life. Remember that you can't change other people; you can only change yourself and the way you perceive situations. Learning to slow down, unplug from technology, and effectively communicate will decrease your stress level. Talking, brainstorming, and looking for solutions to life problems will also help you de-stress. Life is not easy, but looking for ways to take care of yourself in those stressful moments will also help you in everyday living. Remember to find gratitude in your life. There are people and things in your life that bring you joy and peace. Focus on those every day to improve your outlook on life.

Situations and events come up in life, and while you may not have control over these situations, you do have control over how you react to them and your attitude toward what happened. It may take some time to decrease the anger, but lashing out will only fuel the fire and make the situation worse. Find a better way. Most of the time people do not try to hurt one another. When someone is reacting on emotional intensity, it almost always creates a bigger problem and more hurt feelings. Take time, be patient, and breathe! Learn to listen more and talk less. Make your words count. Listen and put yourself in the other person's sandals. Do you hear what he or she is actually saying? Or are you stuck in your own head coming up with a response. Stop it! Listen, breathe, and then respond; you will find your interactions with others are improving. Be mindful and present in your day, don't ignore your mental health, give thanks often, and learn to enjoy life. It is pretty great.

About the Author

Kelly Bawden has had a love of psychology and the mental health field since she was a young child. Her friends and family always knew she would be a therapist someday. She struggled in school most of her life and gave up the dream of psychology in her early 20's. She began raising her children which became her main focus. In 1997 at age 37 her desire to be in the psychology field took over and she began the journey of school and working with teenagers in crisis. She loved what she was doing and worked hard to finish school. Her dream of being a therapist and helping others became a reality and life was good. In 2008 her 26 year old son passed away in a car accident and her world shattered. She was functioning and existing but she was not living. There are times from 2009 to 2011 that were a blur because she was running on auto-pilot just to make it through the day. Her only goal was to get to bed at night and sleep. Sleep had become her coping skill and she used it every chance she got. Eventually she lost her job, endured 5 more deaths in the family and felt lost. The mental health tips in this book have helped many of her clients with their struggles. Now it was her time to put her feet to the fire and do the work that she had helped others do. "Not as easy as I have made it seem" she would tell herself. This is her journey and how she learned to live in spite of the loss that affects her life every day. Mental health matters and these mental health tips work.